South-Western

LOTUS® 1-2-3®
QUICK COURSE

Anita Thompson
BEN DAVIS HIGH SCHOOL
INDIANAPOLIS, IN

SOUTH-WESTERN PUBLISHING CO.

Copyright © 1995

by SOUTH-WESTERN PUBLISHING CO.

Cincinnati, Ohio

ALL RIGHTS RESERVED

I(T)P

International Thomson Publishing

South-Western Publishing Co. is an ITP company. The ITP trademark is used under license.

The text of this publication, or any part thereof, may not be reproduced or transmitted in any form or by any means, electronic or mechanical, including photocopying, recording, storage in an information retrieval system or otherwise, without the prior written permission of the publisher.

ISBN: 0–538–63535–5

2 3 4 5 6 PR 99 98 97 96

Printed in the United States of America

Editor-In-Chief: Bob First

Acquisitions Editor: Janie F. Schwark

Senior Production Editor: Mary Todd

Production Editor: Lois Boggs-Leavens

Designer: Darren Wright

Consulting Editor: John King

Lotus and 1-2-3 are registered trademarks of Lotus Development Corporation.

Preface

Lotus 1-2-3, Quick Course is an easy and enjoyable means of learning a major software package. After twelve to fifteen hours of hands-on application, the novice will have a solid foundation in worksheet, database, and graphic features.

A major goal of this text is to help students learn by doing. As a result, text to read is kept at a minimum, and the text progresses from step-by-step lesson exercises to end-of-lesson reinforcement activities. Directions are written for Lotus 1-2-3 Releases 2.2 through 3.2, with very little release accommodation required.

These instructional materials are suitable for adults or high school students in computer applications, office technology, office procedures, accounting/recordkeeping, and lab courses, among others.

The text is organized into the following lessons:

LESSON 1	Introduction to Spreadsheets
LESSON 2	The Worksheet Screen and Command Menu
LESSON 3	Entering Data
LESSON 4	Retrieve and Print
LESSON 5	Formulas
LESSON 6	Functions
LESSON 7	Range and Global Format
LESSON 8	Advanced Printing
LESSON 9	Changing the Worksheet with Move, Insert, and Delete
LESSON 10	Changing the Worksheet with Copy and Repeat Characters
LESSON 11	Sorting
LESSON 12	Data Queries and Data Fill
LESSON 13	Graphs
LESSON 14	Small Business Application

HELPFUL FEATURES

Each lesson contains the following learning guides:

- An introductory list of lesson objectives.
- A list of vocabulary terms that students will encounter in the lesson.
- Quick Check questions every few pages to check student understanding.
- Many charts for visual learning.
- Screen captures to give students confidence.

End-of-lesson aids include the following:

- New commands and keys.
- New vocabulary.
- Three hands-on reinforcement activities.
- The names of files created in the lesson.

The many reinforcement activities allow an instructor to select some or all for student completion and can provide additional practice for students who work quickly. Critical thinking activities every second lesson are suitable for work teams or individuals.

A comprehensive final activity involves students in various worksheet, database, and graphing activities that require critical thinking skills.

The following reference materials are included at the end of the text:

- A list of 1-2-3 commands and keys.
- A comprehensive glossary.

A template disk is available to accelerate the learning process by reducing the amount of student data entry required. A valuable aid to the instructor is a solutions disk that can be used to replace a lost student file, to visually project a worksheet, or to print cell formulas to check student work. Also, students will frequently use previously completed worksheets in the completion of new work, and the solutions disk can provide files the student has not completed.

An instructor's manual includes teaching hints and timelines, answers to the Quick Check questions, a list of template and solution files, and printed template and solution worksheets.

NOTE TO THE LEARNER

Learning to use new software is a challenging experience! If you have never used a spreadsheet program, Lotus 1-2-3 may seem very different from previous programs you have learned. *Hang in there!* You are learning a skill that millions of people use every day, around the world.

After you become proficient with 1-2-3, you will be able to complete many types of financial projects, both personal and business. Be open to opportunities in which a spreadsheet can help you solve everyday problems.

It is important for you to proceed through the text lessons in the order presented. You will use previously prepared worksheets to complete some activities. Answer the Quick Check questions when you come to them; it is more beneficial to check your understanding right after you have completed the related material. Use the Help feature when you have a question, rather than depending on the assistance of someone else; you will become more resourceful and a more skillful computer user.

ACKNOWLEDGMENTS

I appreciate having editors like Janie and Dave who are so helpful and easy to work with. My consulting editor John deserves special praise for his diligent work to make this book clear and accurate; thanks, John!

Special thanks once again to my husband Terry for generously giving me the time and space to self actualize. And thanks to my daughter Jolie, also a self actualizer; her creativity and courage are an inspiration to me.

Contents

LESSON 1: **Introduction to Spreadsheets** 1
- Objectives 1
- Vocabulary 1
- Why Spreadsheets Are Used 2
- Lotus 1-2-3 Spreadsheet 3
- How 1-2-3 Calculates 3
- Keyboards and 1-2-3 5
- Function Keys and 1-2-3 6
- Mouse 6
- Instructions for Using This Book 6
- Activities 9

LESSON 2: **Worksheet Screen and Command Menu** 11
- Objectives 11
- Vocabulary 11
- Load 1-2-3 12
- The Worksheet 12
- Moving the Pointer 14
- Using the Mouse 16
- The Control Panel 18
- Command Menu 19
- Help Feature 21
- Quit 22
- New Commands and Keys 22
- Activities 25

LESSON 3: **Entering Data** 27
- Objectives 27
- Vocabulary 27
- Correcting Errors 27
- Labels 28
- Numbers 31
- Column Width 32
- Change the Default Drive 33
- Save a Worksheet 34
- Erase a Worksheet 35
- Quit 1-2-3 35

vii

New Commands and Keys	36
Files Created in this Lesson	36
Activities	37
Critical Thinking Project 3	40

LESSON 4: **Retrieve and Print** 41

Objectives	41
Vocabulary	41
Retrieve a Worksheet	41
Replace a Worksheet	42
Print	44
New Commands and Keys	47
Files Created in this Lesson	47
Activities	49

LESSON 5: **Formulas** 51

Objectives	51
Vocabulary	51
Using Numbers and Numeric Systems	51
Special Characters	52
Formulas	53
Edit Cells	56
New Commands and Keys	59
Files Created or Edited in this Lesson	59
Activities	61
Critical Thinking Project 5	64

LESSON 6: **Functions** 65

Objectives	65
Vocabulary	65
Constructing a Function	66
New Commands and Keys	73
Files Created in this Lesson	73
Activities	75

LESSON 7: **Range and Global Format** 79

Objectives	79
Vocabulary	79
Range	79
Erase	80
Format of Numbers	82
Global Format	84
Range Format	85
Format of Labels	88
Global Column Width	89

New Commands and Keys	90
Files Created in this Lesson	90
Activities	91
Critical Thinking Project 7	94

LESSON 8: Advanced Printing — 95

Objectives	95
Vocabulary	95
Wide Worksheets	95
Print Cell Formulas	99
Page Break	100
Borders	101
Headers and Footers	103
Clear Print Settings	103
New Commands and Keys	104
Files Created in this Lesson	105
Activities	107

LESSON 9: Changing the Worksheet with Move, Insert, and Delete — 109

Objectives	109
Vocabulary	109
Move	109
Insert Rows and Columns	112
Undo	114
Delete Rows and Columns	114
Viewing with Windows and Titles	116
Titles	118
New Commands and Keys	120
Files Created in this Lesson	120
Activities	121
Critical Thinking Project 9	124

LESSON 10: Changing the Worksheet with Copy and Repeat Characters — 125

Objectives	125
Vocabulary	125
Copy	125
Copy Labels	126
Copy Formulas	127
Relative Copy	129
Copy Functions	129
Copy Absolute	131
Repeat Characters	133
New Commands and Keys	135

    Files Created in this Lesson 135
    Activities 137

LESSON 11: Sorting 141
    Objectives 141
    Vocabulary 141
    1-2-3 as a Database 141
    Sorting 143
    New Commands and Keys 150
    Files Created in this Lesson 150
    Activities 151
    Critical Thinking Project 11 154

LESSON 12: Data Queries and Data Fill 155
    Objectives 155
    Vocabulary 155
    Data Query 155
    Input Range 156
    Output Range 156
    Criteria Range 156
    Preparing a Database for Query 156
    Data Query Steps 157
    Query Find 158
    Query Delete 164
    Query Extract 165
    Data Fill 168
    New Commands and Keys 170
    Files Created in this Lesson 170
    Activities 171

LESSON 13: Graphs 175
    Objectives 175
    Vocabulary 175
    Graphs 176
    Types of Graphs 176
    Elements of a Graph 177
    Line Graphs 179
    Bar Graphs 185
    Pie Graphs 191
    Graph Reset 191
    Print Graphs 193
    New Commands and Keys 196
    Files Created in this Lesson 196
    Named Graphs in this Lesson 197
    Saved Graphs in this Lesson 197

Activities 199
Critical Thinking Project 13 202

LESSON 14: Advanced Application — Balloon Biz 203
Objectives 203
Your New Position 203
Customer Database 204
Vendor Database... 205
Inventory Record 206
General Journal... 207
Daily Procedure 209
Files Created in this Lesson 216

APPENDIX Lotus 1-2-3 Functions, Special Keys, and Commands...................................... 217
Functions 217
Function Keys 217
Label Prefix Characters....................................... 217
Special Keys 218
Commands... 219

GLOSSARY **222**

INDEX **226**

LESSON 1

Introduction to Spreadsheets

OBJECTIVES

- Define spreadsheet
- Compare a paper accounting form to a spreadsheet
- Describe "playing what if"
- Name the three functions of Lotus 1-2-3
- Calculate formulas using the correct order of operations
- Classify a keyboard as standard or enhanced to select numeric entry
- Tell whether a template or a mouse will be used
- Understand directions for completing the course

Estimated Time: 20 minutes

VOCABULARY

As you learn to use 1-2-3 in this text, new terms will be listed for you at the beginning of each lesson. The terms are arranged in alphabetical order. Definitions for all terms are provided in the Glossary on pages 222–224.

Database	Graph	Program
DOS platform	Num Lock key	Software package
Enhanced keyboard	Numeric keypad	Spreadsheet
Function key	Order of operations	Standard keyboard
Function key template	"Playing what if"	

WHY SPREADSHEETS ARE USED

What do a neighborhood grocery store, a hospital, and a large corporation have in common? For one thing, keeping accurate financial records is crucial for each to stay in business. Each business must know exactly how much money it will receive from customers, how much money it owes to others, the cost of operating expenses, and how much money it has invested. Having this information on a computer for ready access and updating can make a business more competitive.

Most businesses today keep their financial records on a computer through the use of a **program** called a spreadsheet. A **spreadsheet** is a computerized version of a page from a paper accounting book. Since all calculating is done on the computer, spreadsheets have eliminated the need for figuring transactions by using paper, pencils, erasers, and calculators. Figure 1-1 shows data on a multi-column sheet of paper. Figure 1-2 shows the same data

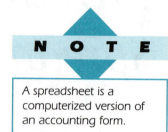

N O T E

A spreadsheet is a computerized version of an accounting form.

Figure 1-1
Manual method of keeping financial records

```
BUSHWHACK TOURS
INCOME AND EXPENSES
199-
                       GROSS                        NET
  TOUR                 INCOME      EXPENSES      INCOME
  Mackinaw Island      22,356       15,899        6,457
  Martha's Vineyard    18,557       12,000        6,557
  Niagara Falls        36,210       28,775        7,435
  San Antonio          55,720       43,665       12,055
  Seattle              28,000       19,993        8,007
  Quebec               64,450       55,231        9,219
  Golden Gate          32,694       22,287       10,407
  Gopher's Gulch       55,721       41,880       13,841
  TOTALS              313,708      239,730       73,978
```

Figure 1-2
Keeping financial records on a computerized spreadsheet

entered in a computerized spreadsheet.

As you can see, a spreadsheet, like an accounting form, is a series of columns and rows in which data can be organized. Most of the data in a spreadsheet is numeric and is used for various mathematical calculations that provide important information. Although the computer can calculate very quickly and accurately, the business owner must construct the appropriate calculations for the computer to perform.

"Playing what if" is used for financial planning.

A spreadsheet is used not only to manage current data, but also as a tool to predict future financial actions. Because spreadsheets can automatically update related figures when a computer user makes a change, one number can be keyed in to see what effect it has on other numbers. This is called **"playing what if."**

Follow the steps below to play a manual version of "what if" with the data in Figure 1-2. Your quest is to answer the following question: Would Bushwhack Tours have a larger net income if they *increased* their gross income by 7% or if they *decreased* their expenses by 10%?

Increasing gross income by 7%:

1. Multiply the Total Gross Income (313,708) by 1.07 (100% of current amount + 7%).
2. From the answer determined in Step 1, subtract the Total Expenses (239,730). This amount is a new Total Net Income.

Decreasing expenses by 10%:

3. Multiply the Total Expenses (239,730) by .90 (100% of current amount − 10%).
4. Subtract the answer determined in Step 3 from the Total Gross Income shown in Figure 1-2 (313,708). This amount is a new Total Net Income.
5. Compare the original Net Income with the figures obtained in Steps 2 and 4. Which would provide the higher net income—increasing gross income by 7% or decreasing expenses by 10%?

LOTUS 1-2-3 SPREADSHEET

Although there are many spreadsheet packages on the market, the most successful one for the **DOS platform** is Lotus 1-2-3. It is called 1-2-3 because it can perform three types of functions: spreadsheet, **graph**, and **database**. You will learn to perform all three of these 1-2-3 functions.

HOW 1-2-3 CALCULATES

Regardless of the **software package** used, computers always calculate in a particular sequence. Therefore, when using 1-2-3 you must enter formulas correctly to receive an accurate solution. Only numeric values can be used in formulas, and the values must be arranged in the proper sequence for a correct solution.

The computer performs calculations from left to right, according to the **order of operations** shown below in Figure 1-3. Expressions in parentheses are calculated first, followed by exponents. Multiplication and division are of equal importance and are performed next. Finally, addition and subtraction, which are of equal importance, are performed.

Values in a formula must be separated by operators, but 1-2-3 does not allow you to put spaces around the operators. The operators (+ – * / ^) are shown with the type of calculation each performs in Figure 1-3.

> **NOTE**
> Only numeric values may be used in formulas.

ORDER OF OPERATIONS

| 1) parentheses ( ) | 2) exponents ^ | 3) multiplication * or division / | 4) addition + or subtraction – |

Figure 1-3
Order of operations for computer calculations.

A sample formula, the steps the computer will use to solve it, and the development of the solution are shown below:

Sample formula: 3 + (9 – 5) * 6 – 2^2

1. Parentheses are solved first:
   (9 – 5) = 4
   The new formula is: 3 + 4 * 6 – 2^2

2. Exponents are solved next.
   2^2 (2 squared or 2 to the second power) = 4
   Now the formula is: 3 + 4 * 6 – 4

3. Multiplication is solved next:
   4 * 6 = 24
   Now the formula is: 3 + 24 – 4

4. Addition is solved next:
   3 + 24 = 27
   The final formula is: 27 – 4 = 23

QUICK QUESTIONS

1. What is a spreadsheet?

2. Compare an accounting paper to a computerized spreadsheet.

   Accounting Paper   *Spreadsheet*

3. What does it mean to "play what if"?

4. List the three functions of Lotus 1-2-3.

   a.

   b.

   c.

5. Sometimes it is better to use an accounting paper and sometimes it is better to use a computerized spreadsheet. Think of several circumstances in which one is a better choice than the other.

   Accounting paper better:

   Computerized spreadsheet better:

KEYBOARDS AND 1-2-3

The type of computer keyboard you are equipped with will determine the way in which you will key numbers. Two types of computer keyboards are available: **standard** and **enhanced**. If your keyboard is enhanced, you can use the cursor keys on the special keypad located between the alphabetic keyboard and the **numeric keypad**. Press the **Num Lock key** to use the numeric pad for the frequent keying of numbers. Figure 1-4 shows the location of the numeric keypad and the Num Lock key on the enhanced keyboard.

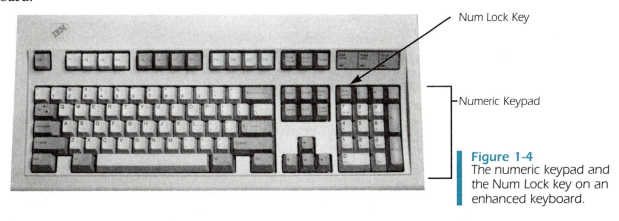

Figure 1-4
The numeric keypad and the Num Lock key on an enhanced keyboard.

If you have a standard keyboard, do not use Num Lock. Use the numeric keypad for cursor movement. When you wish to key a number, press Shift while pressing the numeric keypad number key. You may also use the numeric keys at the top of the alphabetic keyboard.

FUNCTION KEYS AND 1-2-3

When using 1-2-3, you will seldom be asked to use a **function key**. If a **template** of function key commands is available, it is helpful but not necessary. Although 1-2-3 makes use of nearly twenty commands on ten function keys, only the ones shown in Figure 1-5 will be used in this text. A list of all function key commands is provided in the Appendix.

Function Key	Purpose
F1	Help
F2	Edit
F4	Absolute
Alt-F4	Undo
F5	Goto
F6	Window
F7	Query
F10	Graph

Figure 1-5
Function keys used in this text.

MOUSE

Beginning with Release 2.3, Lotus 1-2-3 supports a mouse. The mouse can be used for pointer movement, command selection, and range setting. Directions for using the mouse are provided in Lesson 2.

INSTRUCTIONS FOR USING THIS BOOK

The following explanation will aid you in working through the activities in this book.

- Text to be keyed, keys to be pressed, and other keyboard/mouse actions will be shown in the exercises with enumerated steps. A notation in brackets indicates the cell in which the activity will take place. Do not key a bracketed notation.

Point to E6

The above direction means move the pointer to cell E6 using the keyboard or mouse.

[C4] PRACTICE WORKSHEET

This means move the pointer to cell C4 and then key the words PRACTICE WORKSHEET.

- Keys to press are shown in keycaps; for example, **END**. If a key is to be held down while you press another one, the keys will be "locked" together: **CTRL**-**←**.

[D12] **F2**

The above direction means move the pointer to cell D12 and then press the F2 function key.

- You may choose to use a mouse instead of the keyboard for many actions. Actions that can be carried out by using a mouse are shown with a mouse picture ().

- Keys to press for commands are shown in bold capital letters. For example:

[A27] / **W**orksheet **G**lobal **F**ormat **C**urrency **2** **ENTER**

The above direction means move the pointer to cell A27 and then press the keys / W G F C 2 **ENTER**. Use upper or lower case for command keys.

A mouse user would move the mouse to the control panel, click on the commands Worksheet, Global, Format, and Currency, key 2, and then click the left button (for Enter).

- Filenames are shown in all caps but may be keyed in either upper or lower case.

- Commands in 1-2-3 Releases 2.x and 3.x are nearly identical. The few exceptions will be shown in italics.

> **NOTE**
>
> The mouse can be used to move the pointer, select commands, and set ranges.

QUICK QUESTIONS

1. Will you use the Num Lock key when entering numbers?
2. Will you have a template or a mouse available?
3. What three actions can a mouse perform in 1-2-3?

    a.

    b.

    c.

4. What action should you take if you see the following direction: [F6] TOTAL SALES?
5. What action should you take if you see the following direction: [D10] / Worksheet Global Column-Width 12 ENTER ?

ACTIVITIES

ACTIVITY 1-1

As a review for working with figures and formulas, calculate the solutions for the following problems. Follow the order of operations shown in Figure 1-3. Write both the formula and the answer in the spaces provided below. Use a calculator or scrap paper if you wish.

1. 3^2 / 3 + (28 + 17) * 5 =

2. 267 – (8 * 2.25) * 12.5 + (66.75 – 23.4) =

3. Find the difference between 3,655.27 and 2,897.82.

4. Find the sum: 782.88, 951.74, 68.22, 5,324.41.

5. Find the average of the following test scores:
   78, 88, 90, 84, 82.

6. A business has sales of $621,890 and expenses of $495,339. What is the gross profit?

7. A salesperson sells $860,000 of product and earns 7% commission on sales. What is the amount of the commission?

LESSON 2

Worksheet Screen and Command Menu

OBJECTIVES

- Load 1-2-3
- Identify rows and columns that intersect as cells
- Identify areas of the worksheet, including the control panel
- Move the pointer
- Activate the command menu and choose commands
- Use the Help and Quit commands
- Cancel commands

Estimated Time: 45 minutes

VOCABULARY

Cell	Cursor keys	Pointer
Cell address	Goto	Row
Column	Home key	Row border
Column border	Home position	Scroll arrows
Command menu	Icon panel	Status Line
Contents line	Main command	Sub command
Control panel	Mode indicator	Toggle
Current Cell	Mouse pointer	Worksheet

LOAD 1-2-3

The place where the 1-2-3 program is stored varies among computer systems. One of the following may load the program for you; otherwise, ask your instructor.

1. Two disk drives:
   a. Start DOS.
   b. Insert the System Disk in drive A.
   c. Insert your data disk in drive B.
   d. Key **b:** [ENTER] to set drive b as the default for files.
   e. Key **a:123** [ENTER] to start 1-2-3.
2. Hard disk:
   a. At the DOS prompt, key **cd\lotus** [ENTER] (or the name of the directory where the Lotus system files are located).
   b. Insert your data diskette in the floppy drive.
   c. Key **123** [ENTER] to start 1-2-3.
3. Networked system:
   a. Log on to the computer system.
   b. Select Lotus 1-2-3 from the menu (or follow instructor directions).

THE WORKSHEET

Load 1-2-3 now, following the steps described above or the directions of your instructor.

▶ **EXERCISE 2-1**

The 1-2-3 worksheet appears, ready for data to be entered. The areas of the worksheet you can see on your screen are similar to those shown in Figure 2-1 (for Release 2.3).

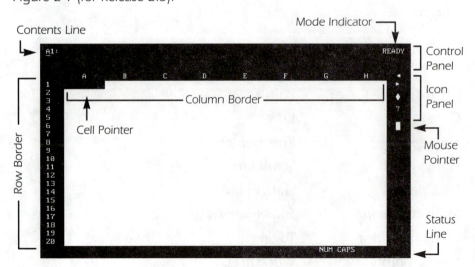

Figure 2-1
The Blank Worksheet

12 LESSON 2 WORKSHEET SCREEN AND COMMAND MENU

COLUMNS AND ROWS

The worksheet uses vertical **columns** and horizontal **rows**, like the accountant's ruled paper.

Columns are vertical, rows are horizontal.

BORDERS

Find the **column border**, a horizontal line of letters across the worksheet that identifies each column. Each letter in the column border refers to the column below it. Only columns A through H are visible on your screen at this time.

The **row border** is a line of numbers going down the left edge of the worksheet that identifies each row. Each number in the row border refers to the row beside it. Only rows 1 through 20 are currently visible.

Only a tiny portion of the worksheet can be seen at once.

There are many more letters in the column border and numbers in the row border than you can see on your screen at one time. The worksheet contains 256 columns and 8,192 rows.

CELLS

Data is keyed at the intersection of a column and a row, which is known as a **cell**. Each cell is identified by a **cell address**, consisting of the column letter and row number of the intersection point. For example, cell address B6 is at the intersection of column B and row 6. Cell C2 is at the intersection of column C and row 2. The column letter is always specified *first* in a cell address. There are over two million cells in a worksheet.

POINTER

The 1-2-3 cursor is rectangular and is called the **pointer**. The pointer adjusts to the size of the cell it is in. In Figure 2-1 and on your worksheet the pointer is in *cell A1*, the place where column A intersects with row 1. The cell that the pointer is on at a particular time is known as the **current cell**. The current cell now is A1.

STATUS LINE

At the bottom of your screen is the **status line**. It displays the date and time, the name of the current worksheet, and other items (such as NUM when Num Lock is on, CAPS when Caps Lock is on, and SCROLL when Scroll Lock is on). The Num Lock, Caps Lock, and Scroll Lock keys are **toggles**; press them to turn the appropriate feature on or off.

Release 3.x Multiple Worksheets: Because 1-2-3 Release 3.x is designed to manage more than one worksheet at a time, the contents line displays a worksheet letter in addition to the current cell or row. Since you will only use one worksheet at a time in this book, the letter A followed by a colon will always precede the column letter and row number of each cell address. Ignore the beginning A: as you follow directions in this book.

QUICK QUESTIONS

1. Are worksheet columns horizontal or vertical?
2. Are worksheet rows horizontal or vertical?
3. What is the term for the line of letters across the worksheet that designates columns?
4. What is the term for the line of numbers down the left side of the worksheet that designates rows?
5. What term refers to the intersection of a column and a row?
6. What term refers to the column letter and row number that identifies a particular cell?
7. How many cells are on a worksheet?
8. What is the term for the 1-2-3 cursor?
9. What term refers to the cell that the pointer is on at a particular time?
10. What term refers to the bottom line of the 1-2-3 screen where the date, time, Num Lock, and similar items are displayed?

MOVING THE POINTER

Even if you have a mouse available, it is helpful to know the keys that will move the pointer. You can then select the technique that will enable you to complete your work more quickly.

HOME

The **Home** key moves the pointer to the upper left corner (cell A1), which is known as the **home position**.

N O T E

Press Home to return to cell A1 from any cell in the worksheet.

CURSOR KEYS

The **cursor keys** are used to move up, down, right, and left one row or column. **Tab** moves the pointer *right* to the next screenful of cells. **Shift-Tab** moves the pointer *left* to the next screenful of cells. **Page Down** moves the pointer *down* a screenful of cells, and **Page Up** moves the pointer *up* a screenful of cells. Tab, Shift-Tab, Page Up, and Page Down move you to the next screenful of cells regardless of the position of the pointer when the key is pressed.

Move around the worksheet.

1. Press **HOME** to be sure A1 is the current cell.
2. Press **→** 5 times to move the pointer five cells to the right of cell A1.
3. Look at the Contents Line. The current cell is F1.
4. Press **↓** 6 times to move the pointer down six cells. What is the current cell?
5. Press **←** 3 times. What is the current cell?
6. Press **HOME** to return to cell A1.
7. Press **TAB**. What is the current cell?
8. Press **SHIFT**–**TAB**. What is the current cell?
9. Press **PAGE DN**. What is the current cell?
10. Press **PAGE UP**. In what **direction** and **how far** does **Page Up** move the pointer?

GOTO

F5 lets you utilize the **Goto** feature, which allows you to quickly move the pointer to any cell. When F5 is pressed, the contents line will ask for an address to go to while it displays the current address. Just key the desired cell address and then press **ENTER**. The cell you choose to go to becomes the cell address displayed in the upper left corner of the screen.

> **NOTE**
>
> F5, the Goto key, is most useful when moving around in a large worksheet.

END

The **End** key is used with a cursor key to quickly move to the most distant row or column in the worksheet. Press End and the **↓** cursor key to move to the last row. The End key and the **→** cursor key move the pointer to the last column in the worksheet.

Go to cell M37.

1. Press **F5** and then key **M** **3** **7** **ENTER**.

Now try the Goto feature yourself.

2. Use Goto to quickly move your cursor to cell A1. What did you press to quickly move to cell A1?

What single key can you press to quickly move to cell A1?

Move to the end of the worksheet.

3. Key **END** **↓**. What is the last row number of the worksheet?
4. Key **END** **→**. What is the last column letter of the worksheet?
5. Press **HOME** to return to cell A1.

QUICK QUESTIONS

1. What is the home position?
2. Which key moves the pointer to A1?
3. Which key moves the cursor to the left, one cell at a time?
4. Which key(s) moves the pointer to the left, one screenful of cells?
5. Which key(s) moves the pointer up, one screenful of cells?
6. Which key is the Goto key?
7. Write the 3 steps necessary to goto cell S88:

    a.

    b.

    c.

8. Which key is used with a cursor key to move to the farthest row or column of the worksheet?

USING THE MOUSE

The mouse is supported for several actions in 1-2-3 Release 2.3 and later. When you have a mouse available, your screen will have two pointers. The cursor bar, known as the **pointer** in 1-2-3, is the size of the cell it occupies. A tiny rectangular **mouse pointer** is also visible on the worksheet.

An **icon panel** for mouse users is provided at the right edge of the screen. This panel contains pictures of screen **scroll arrows** (◄►▲▼) and a question mark (?) as a symbol for Help. *Release 3.x has additional ↑ and ↓ icons used for multiple worksheets; ignore these. Release 2.4 has a unique icon panel; some of the directions given here may not apply.*

Figure 2-2 shows how to use the mouse icons for pointer movement and help, and how to use the mouse itself to select commands and act as Enter or Esc. For example, to move the pointer down one row, place the mouse pointer on the ▼ symbol on the icon panel, and then click (press) the left mouse button. Each time you click on the symbol, the pointer will move down a row. To move down many rows, hold down the left mouse button until you reach the desired row.

Action	Mouse Operation
Move pointer to a specific cell	Move the mouse pointer to the desired cell and then click the left mouse button.
Move pointer left	Point to ◄ on the icon panel and click or hold down the left mouse button.
Move pointer right	Point to ► on the icon panel and click or hold down the left mouse button.
Move pointer up	Point to ▲ on the icon panel and click or hold down the left mouse button.
Move pointer down	Point to ▼ on the icon panel and click or hold down the left mouse button.
Help	Point to ? on the icon panel and click the left mouse button.
Enter	Click the left mouse button.
Esc	Click the right mouse button.
Select a command	Point to the command name and click the left mouse button.

Figure 2-2
Mouse Actions.

If you have a mouse available as you work through this text, you may choose to use the mouse instead of the keyboard whenever possible. Mouse actions are described in the margin beside the keyboard actions when a new activitity is presented; they are indicated with the mouse picture . Since you will quickly learn to use the mouse, mouse actions are not given for all keyboard explanations.

You can see in Figure 2-2 that the left mouse button is used for all actions except Esc to cancel. As you follow directions, use the left mouse button for all actions unless told specifically to use the right button.

► **EXERCISE 2-4**

If you have a mouse, complete the following actions:

1. Click on the icon panel's screen scroll arrows with the mouse button to move the pointer and change the current cell.

2. Return to cell A1 by clicking on the screen scroll arrows until the pointer returns to cell A1.

THE CONTROL PANEL

The three top lines of the 1-2-3 screen, above the column border, are referred to as the control panel. The **control panel** keeps you informed of the current cell address, the contents and other characteristics of the current cell, and the current operating mode. When you use a 1-2-3 command, the command menu will appear on the control panel.

> **NOTE**
>
> The control panel keeps you informed about the current cell and operating mode, and it displays the command menu.

CONTENTS LINE

The current cell address (A1) appears in the top left corner of the control panel. The line that contains this information is known as **the contents line**. The contents line also displays the contents and format of the current cell when the current cell contains data.

> **NOTE**
>
> The contents line displays the current cell address and the contents and format of the current cell.

MODE INDICATOR

The current operating mode (Ready) appears in the upper right corner of the control panel. This is known as the **mode indicator**. You can enter new data only when the mode indicator shows Ready.

> **NOTE**
>
> You can enter new data only when the mode indicator displays **Ready**.

Watch the contents line for the current cell as you move the pointer. Begin at cell A1.

1. Press → and ↓ to move around the worksheet.
2. Return the pointer to cell A1.

Watch the status line for the condition of toggles.

3. Press **NUM LOCK**, **SCROLL LOCK**, and **CAPS LOCK** to turn the toggles on.
4. Now turn the toggles off.

▶ **EXERCISE 2–5**

Click on the screen scroll arrows to move around the worksheet.

QUICK QUESTIONS

1. What is the term for the top three lines of the 1-2-3 screen, which keep you informed of the current cell address, the contents and other characteristics of the current cell, and the current operating mode?

2. What term refers to the control panel line that displays the current cell address, as well as its contents and format?

3. What is the term for the upper right corner of the control panel that displays the current operating mode?

COMMAND MENU

1-2-3 has easy-to-use commands that are displayed step by step on the screen. When a main command is chosen, its sub command menu appears. A **main command** is any of the commands that appear on the first line of commands when the command menu is activated.

A **sub command** is a command choice that is a result of the previous command selected. When a first level sub command is chosen, a second level of sub command choices then appears. This process is repeated until the command is completed. A list of 1-2-3 commands is included at the end of this text.

The list below shows how the command menu progresses step by step, level by level. The command to insert a column into a worksheet would require the following main command and sub commands:

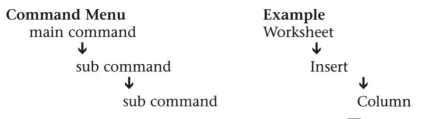

The **command menu** is activated by pressing the [/] key or by moving the mouse pointer to the control panel.

Press [/] to activate the command menu.

The command menu occupies two lines of the control panel, below the current cell (A1) and the mode indicator (Menu). As shown in Figure 2-3, the second line of the control panel displays the main command menu, and the third line displays a sub command menu. The Worksheet command is highlighted at this time, so you see the sub commands available for that main command.

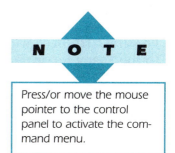

Press/or move the mouse pointer to the control panel to activate the command menu.

 EXERCISE 2-6

Move the mouse pointer to the control panel.

Figure 2-3
The Command Menu.

After activating the command menu, press → to move to other main commands so you can view their corresponding sub commands.

CHOOSING A COMMAND

When the command menu is displayed, a command may be chosen in several ways: by moving the pointer to the command and pressing Enter, by pressing the first letter of the command, or by clicking the mouse button on the command name. Pressing the first letter of the command is usually the quickest method.

NOTE: To quickly select a command, press the first letter of the command.

BACK OUT OF OR CANCEL A COMMAND

If you start a command and change your mind or press the wrong key, you may back out one step at a time or entirely cancel the command you have started. Each time you press Esc or click the *right* mouse button, you will back out one command level. Pressing Ctrl-Break will cancel the entire command and return you to the Ready mode. (Break is located on the Pause key.)

NOTE: Back out of a command one level at a time with Esc or the right mouse button. Cancel a command in one step with Ctrl-Break.

QUICK QUESTIONS

1. Which key activates the command menu?
2. What is a 1-2-3 sub command?
3. List three methods of choosing a command when the command menu is displayed.
   a.
   b.
   c.
4. What key is pressed to back out of a command one step at a time?
5. What keys are pressed to cancel an entire command?

Practice backing out of and canceling commands.

1. Press **CTRL**–**BREAK** to cancel any current command and return to Ready mode.
2. Key / **W**orksheet **I**nsert

▶ **EXERCISE 2-8**

Move to the control panel and then click on Worksheet, Insert.

Back out of the command one level at a time.

3. Press [ESC] 3 times.

Click the **right** mouse button 3 times.

Begin the command again and then cancel it.

4. Key / **W**orksheet **I**nsert

Move to the control panel and then click on Worksheet, Insert.

5. Press [CTRL]–[BREAK] to cancel the command.

HELP FEATURE

To find out more about commands or other features of the program, get **Help** by pressing F1 or clicking the mouse button on the question mark (?) on the icon panel. You can obtain Help before you begin a command or while you are in the process of building a command. Cancel the Help screen when desired by pressing the [ESC] key or clicking the *right* mouse button.

Press F1 to access Help. Press Esc or click the right mouse button to cancel Help.

▶ **EXERCISE 2-9**

Use the Help feature.

1. Look at the upper right corner of the control panel to be sure you are out of the Menu mode and in Ready mode. If not, press [CTRL]–[BREAK].

2. When you are in Ready mode, press [F1] to access Help.

The 1-2-3 Help Index appears.

Click the mouse button on the ? on the icon panel.

3. Spend some time learning to scroll through Help to get information about the various 1-2-3 features. Press [ESC] to cancel Help when desired.

Activate the command menu to get Help about a specific command.

4. Key [/].

The main command **Worksheet** is highlighted. Below the main command line are the sub commands that are available if you choose Worksheet: Global, Insert, Delete, Column, Erase, Titles, Window, Status, Page, Learn. Find out more about the Worksheet sub command **Window**.

Move the mouse to the control panel.

5. Key [w] for Worksheet.

The sub commands have moved up to line two on the Control Panel and now have their own sub commands.

Click on Worksheet.

6. Move the menu pointer to highlight **Window**.

7. Key [F1] for Help.

8. What does the **W**orksheet **W**indow command do, according to the Help screen?

Click the mouse button on the ? symbol.

9. After pressing / **W**orksheet **W**indow, highlight **Vertical** and then press [F1] for Help. What is the purpose of Vertical Window?

LESSON 2 WORKSHEET SCREEN AND COMMAND MENU **21**

10. Press **ESC** to exit **H**elp.

Press **CTRL**–**BREAK** to cancel the command menu and return to Ready mode.

Click the **right** mouse button to exit Help.

Use the Help feature when you have questions or are just curious about a command. Always access the Help feature for solutions before asking your instructor for help.

QUIT

Use the **Quit** command to exit properly from 1-2-3 and return to the system prompt or program menu. WARNING: When you wish to store your work, you must use the File Save command before choosing the Quit command. You will learn to use the save command and store your work in Lesson 3. If you do not save your worksheet, you will receive a warning message; press *y* for *Yes* to verify Quit without saving if that is appropriate.

When your work session is over, exit 1-2-3.

Key / **Q**uit **Y**es (**Y**es to verify if asked).

▶ **EXERCISE 2–10**

Click on **Q**uit, **Y**es, (**Y**es to verify if asked).

QUICK QUESTIONS

1. What key is pressed to get Help?
2. What key is pressed to cancel Help?
3. What keys are pressed to exit from 1-2-3?
4. Does using the Quit command store your worksheet?

NEW COMMANDS AND KEYS

HOME. Returns the pointer to cell A1.

Cursor keys. Move the pointer up, down, left, and right.

TAB. Moves the pointer right to the next screenful of cells.

SHIFT–**TAB**. Moves the pointer left to the next screenful of cells.

PAGE DN. Moves the pointer down to the next screenful of cells.

PAGE UP. Moves the pointer up to the next screenful of cells.

F5. The Goto feature; it allows quick movement to a specified cell.

END. Used with a cursor key to go to the farthest point of the worksheet.

N O T E

The Quit command does not save your worksheet.

ESC. Cancels current keying or moves one step back in a command. Also backs out of a command one level at a time.

/. Activates the command menu.

CTRL–**BREAK**. Cancels an entire command.

F1. Activates Help.

/Quit Yes (Yes). Exits 1-2-3 without storing the worksheet.

ACTIVITIES

Identify the parts of the following worksheet. Write the name of the part beside its corresponding letter. Try to recall each part yourself, but use Figure 2-1 if needed.

ACTIVITY 2-1

1.   5.
2.   6.
3.   7.
4.   8.

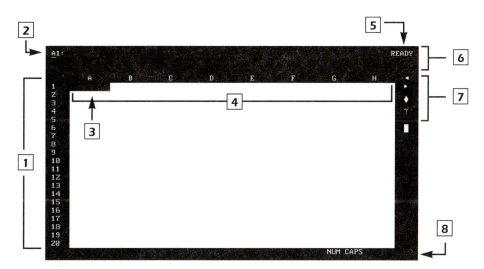

Load 1-2-3 if necessary. Carefully follow the directions below to move the pointer around the worksheet. When you have completed all of the indicated movements, note which cell is the current cell.

ACTIVITY 2-2

1. Begin at cell A1.
2. Press [TAB].
3. Press [PAGE DN] twice.
4. Press [→] 5 times.
5. Press [↓] 6 times.
6. Press [SHIFT]–[TAB].
7. Press [PAGE UP].
8. Press [END] [→].
9. What is the current cell?

ACTIVITY 2-3

Use the Help feature to get information about entering data as numbers in a worksheet. List three of the facts you discover in the spaces provided.

1.

2.

3.

LESSON 3

Entering Data

OBJECTIVES

- Correct miskeying
- Enter labels and use label prefix characters
- Enter labels that begin with a number
- Enter numbers
- Set column width
- Set default drive
- Save a worksheet
- Erase a worksheet

Estimated Time: 30 minutes

VOCABULARY

Default	Label	Path
Drive	Label prefix character	Spill over
File extension	Numeric symbol	Value

CORRECTING ERRORS

As you enter data, you may make errors of different kinds. Refer to Figure 3-1 when you need to correct or cancel miskeyed information, cancel commands you have started, or make a cell blank. Notice, particularly, that the Esc key/right mouse button is used to correct several types of errors.

ERROR CORRECTION CHART

Error	Keying Status	Correction
Miskeyed data	Currently keying in that cell	1. Backspace to erase and **rekey** or 2. Press **Esc** or the right mouse button to cancel the keyed data and then rekey
	Have moved to a different cell	1. Go back to the cell in error and **rekey** or 2. Go back to the cell in error and press **F2** to edit
Keyed data in a cell that should be blank	Currently keying in that cell	Press **Esc** or the right mouse button to cancel the keyed data
	Have moved to a different cell	Go back to the cell in error and press **Delete** or use the **Range Erase** command
Miskeyed a command	Currently keying	Press **Esc** or the right mouse button to take one step back
	Have moved on	Go through the command again, choosing the correct option

Figure 3-1
Error Correction Chart.

The Esc key is used to cancel a command level or to cancel data being entered.

QUICK QUESTIONS

1. If you miskey data that you are currently entering in a cell, what are two methods you can use to correct it?

    a.

    b.

2. If you keyed data in a cell that should be blank and you have moved to a different cell, what should you do?

3. If you miskey the command you are currently entering, how can you go back a step in the command menu?

LABELS

A text entry, called a **label**, consists of alphabetic characters or a mixture of letters, symbols, and numbers. When you key a letter as the first character in a cell, 1-2-3 assumes you are keying a label and automatically precedes the label with an apostrophe. (The 1-2-3 default designator of a label is an apostrophe.)

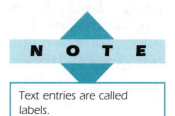

Text entries are called labels.

As you enter data into the worksheet, remember that [A1] means to move the pointer to cell A1 and then key. Use Figure 3-1 for help in correcting errors.

Watch the changes on the control panel as you key.

1. Load 1-2-3.
2. [A1] PARTY FOODS AND PRICES (Do not press **ENTER**.)
3. [A1] Look at the mode indicator to verify that the current mode is LABEL.
4. [A1] **ENTER**.
5. [A1] Look at the contents line to verify that there is an apostrophe in front of the label PARTY FOODS AND PRICES.

SPILL OVER

The heading you keyed at A1 extends beyond the cell and **spills over** into the blank cells on the right, B1 and C1. If the cells to the right of the label contained data, the label would not be visible in its entirety; it would look cut off.

LABEL PREFIX CHARACTERS

The apostrophe in front of the *P* in PARTY at cell A1 is the default **label prefix character**. A label prefix character determines where a label will be aligned in a cell. The apostrophe as a label prefix character aligns a label at the *left* of the cell. The label PARTY FOODS AND PRICES is aligned at the left of cell A1, as designated by the apostrophe. Every label will have either the default label prefix character or one you select.

Figure 3-2 shows the label prefix characters and the positions they determine.

▶ **EXERCISE 3-1**

Move the mouse to the control panel and then click the left mouse button.

Long labels will spill over into blank cells at the right of the label.

The default label alignment is at the left of a cell, achieved by preceding the label with an apostrophe.

LABEL PREFIX CHARACTERS	
'	Aligns at the left of the cell (default)
"	Aligns at the right of the cell
^	Aligns at the center of the cell

Figure 3-2
Label Prefix Characters.

A LABEL THAT BEGINS WITH A NUMBER

When a cell entry begins with a number but is followed with letters or non-numeric symbols, you must tell 1-2-3 to treat it as a label. To do this, press the desired label prefix character (usually the apostrophe) before the number. As with all labels, the entry cannot be used in calculations. Examples of labels that begin with a number are addresses, telephone numbers, and stock numbers.

> **N O T E**
>
> Any entry that begins with a number but contains letters or non-numeric characters must be preceded by a label prefix character.

QUICK QUESTIONS

1. What is the term for text entries?
2. What does 1-2-3 do with a label that is too wide for its column if the cells to the right are empty?
3. What does 1-2-3 do with a label that is too wide for its column if the cells to the right contain data?
4. What is the term for the special symbol in front of a label that determines its alignment in a cell?
5. Where in a cell is a label aligned by default?
6. Where will the quotes (") label prefix character align a label in a cell?
7. What must precede a label that begins with a number?

As you key the labels below, precede them with label prefix characters where indicated. Key in upper and lower case as shown. Do *not* press Enter after you key each entry; just key the entry and then press the cursor key(s) that will take you to the next cell for entry. Pressing a cursor key completes an entry and moves in the desired direction in one step.

> **N O T E**
>
> After keying data in a cell, press a cursor key rather than Enter.

EXERCISE 3-2

1. Add the following data to the heading you keyed at cell A1. You may use the cursor keys shown or the mouse icons to move the pointer to each cell for label entry.

   [A3] [^] FOOD (Centers the label.)
   [A3] [→]
   [B3] [^] AMOUNT (Centers the label.)
   [B3] [→]
   [C3] ["] PRICES (Right aligns the label.)
   [C3] [↓] [↓] [←] [←] (Moves the pointer to cell A5.)
   [A5] Chips
   [A5] [↓]
   Press the [↓] cursor key after the four entries below.
   [A6] Cheese
   [A7] Crackers
   [A8] Punch
   [A9] Cookies
   [A10] Pretzels [ENTER]
   [A10] [F5] [b] [5] [ENTER]

30   LESSON 3   ENTERING DATA

2. Enter labels that begin with numbers by preceding them with the apostrophe label prefix character. Press the [↓] cursor key after each entry below.

[B5]   ['] 1 bag
[B6]   ['] 1 pound
[B7]   ['] 1 box
[B8]   ['] 4 cans
[B9]   ['] 1 dozen
[B10] ['] 1 bag

3. Keep this worksheet on your screen for the next exercise.

NUMBERS

When you key a numeric digit or **numeric symbol** as the first character of a cell, 1-2-3 assumes you are entering a *number* or *formula* and will display **Value** on the mode indicator. Only numeric values can be calculated. Numeric symbols include the plus sign, minus sign, decimal point (period), and parenthesis. Numbers may not be preceded by $, #, @, or any other symbol not considered a numeric symbol. *Numbers must be allowed to align on the right of a cell without a label prefix character.*

> **NOTE**
>
> Numbers may only be preceded by the following symbols: a plus or minus sign, a decimal point, or a parenthesis.

APPEARANCE OF NUMBERS

Except for necessary decimal points and minus signs for negative numbers, you *do not* control the appearance of numbers when you key them. For example, unnecessary zeros will not be displayed. Later in this text you will use commands to format numbers for better appearance.

> **NOTE**
>
> Unless formatted, numbers will not diplay unnecessary zeros.

QUICK QUESTIONS

1. What appears on the mode indicator when you are keying a number?

2. What is the only type of data that can be calculated?

3. List the four numeric symbols that may precede a number in a value.

   a.

   b.

   c.

   d.

4. Numbers must align on which side of a cell?

Enter numbers into the worksheet.

1. Move the pointer to cell C5.
2. Press the [↓] cursor key after each entry below.

    [C5]   2.50
    [C6]   3.99
    [C7]   2.39
    [C8]   4.99
    [C9]   2.99
    [C10]   1.70 **ENTER**

Your worksheet should look like Figure 3-3. Keep the worksheet on your screen.

▶ **EXERCISE 3-3**

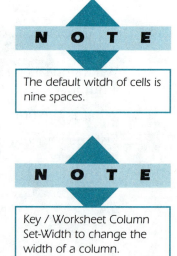

```
         A         B         C         D         E
 1  PARTY FOODS AND PRICES
 2
 3      FOOD      AMOUNT    PRICES
 4
 5  Chips     1 bag          2.5
 6  Cheese    1 pound        3.99
 7  Crackers  1 box          2.39
 8  Punch     4 cans         4.99
 9  Cookies   1 dozen        2.99
10  Pretzels  1 bag          1.7
11
12
```

Figure 3-3
Worksheet Check.

COLUMN WIDTH

The default (specification set by the software writers) width of cells is *nine* spaces. You can change the width of a cell, but that will affect the *entire column* the cell is in. For example, if you widen cell D5 to 12 spaces, you will widen all of column D to 12 spaces. Do not widen columns to accommodate main headings; widen columns only for column headings and column data.

If the default width of a column is changed, a number in brackets on the contents line indicates the new size of the column. For example, when at a cell in a column you have widened, [W12] indicates a width of 12. If no width indication appears, the column still has the default size of nine spaces (or a global column width has been specified, as you will do in Lesson 7).

Use the **Worksheet Column Set-Width** command to widen all cells in one column. The pointer can be at any cell in the column when you use the command.

NOTE

The default witdh of cells is nine spaces.

NOTE

Key / Worksheet Column Set-Width to change the width of a column.

With the party food list on your screen, change the width of column A to 12 spaces.

1. Move the pointer so that any cell in column A is the current cell.
2. Press **/** to activate the command menu.

To complete commands with the keyboard, press the first letter of each word in the command; the letters are shown in bold. You will press **w** **c** **s** **1** **2** **ENTER** to complete the command shown below:

3. Key **W**orksheet **C**olumn **S**et-Width **1** **2** **ENTER**.

Note that the contents line shows [W12] for **width of 12**.

4. Move the pointer to any cell in column C. Use the steps above to set a column width of 7 spaces for all cells in column C. Look for [W7] on the contents line.

When using the Worksheet Column Set-Width command, you can press the → or ← keys until the column is a desirable width instead of keying a particular character width. You will use this method later.

> ▶ **EXERCISE 3-4**
>
>
>
> Move the mouse pointer to the control panel.
>
>
>
> Click on Worksheet, Column, Set-Width, key <1> <2>, and click the left mouse button.
>
>
>
> To widen a column, key the width in numbers or press the left or right cursor key until the desired width is attained.

QUICK QUESTIONS

1. What is the default size of a cell?
2. What notation would appear on the contents line if you widened a cell to 15 spaces?
3. What do you know about the width of a cell if there is no width indication?
4. Where should the pointer be if you wish to widen column C?
5. Write the command you would key to change a column width to 10.

CHANGE THE DEFAULT DRIVE

You will save keying time and avoid possible file storage problems if you use a command to designate the drive and **path** for storing your 1-2-3 worksheets, thereby changing the **default drive** for your program or your computer. This drive specification and directory can be a temporary or a permanent setting.

A temporary directory setting is in effect for the current work session only. A permanent directory setting will remain in effect for all 1-2-3 sessions.

LESSON 3 ENTERING DATA

TEMPORARY DIRECTORY

Use the **File Directory** command to set a temporary directory *each time* you use 1-2-3. The drive and path you key will depend on whether you save your work on a diskette, fixed disk, or network file server. A temporary directory is set with the following command:

/ File Directory *drive and path* ENTER

PERMANENT DIRECTORY

Use the **Worksheet Global Default Directory** command to set a permanent directory that will remain in effect for your computer. The drive and path you key will depend on whether you save your work on a diskette, fixed disk, or network file server. A permanent directory is set with the following command:

/ Worksheet Global Default Directory *drive and path* ENTER
  Update Quit

Place a check mark in front of the directory specification your instructor wants you to use.

_____ Temporary Directory   _____ Permanent Directory

In the space below, write what you should key to set your directory. Your instructor will tell you what to key for the path.

Key the command you wrote above for setting your directory.

SAVE A WORKSHEET

Once the default drive is set, the **File Save** command is used to store the worksheet on disk. When using 1-2-3, do *not* give files a **file extension**. 1-2-3 automatically gives all worksheets the file extension .WK1 in Release 2.x and .WK3 in Release 3.x. A standard file extension makes 1-2-3 worksheets recognizable by both computer users and the 1-2-3 program when the File Retrieve command is used.

To save the practice worksheet on your disk, key the first letter of each command step (shown in bold) in the next exercise. The file name PRAC3 is shown in upper case, but you may key it in lower case.

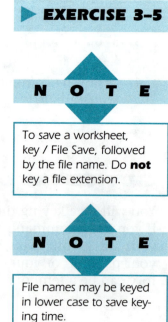

▶ **EXERCISE 3-5**

N O T E

To save a worksheet, key / File Save, followed by the file name. Do **not** key a file extension.

N O T E

File names may be keyed in lower case to save keying time.

Save the party food worksheet. Be sure you have set the directory so your worksheet will store in the desired place.

1. Press **/** to activate the command menu.
2. Key **F**ile **S**ave PRAC3 **ENTER**

1-2-3 saved the file, and the mode indicator now displays *Ready*. The worksheet, however, remains on your screen. After saving a worksheet on disk, use the Worksheet Erase command to get a new, clean worksheet, or use the Quit command to exit from 1-2-3.

ERASE A WORKSHEET

To erase a worksheet from the screen, use the **Worksheet Erase** command. Remember to save your worksheet before using this command! 1-2-3 may ask you to verify before completing the command to help you avoid an accidental erasure.

QUIT 1-2-3

When your work session is over, use the **Quit** command to exit properly from Lotus 1-2-3. Save your worksheet before using this command. You will be prompted to verify quitting if you have not saved the current worksheet. (It is not necessary to erase a worksheet before exiting 1-2-3.)

▶ **EXERCISE 3-6**

Move the mouse pointer to the control panel.

Click on **F**ile, **S**ave, key PRAC3, click the left mouse button.

Erasing a worksheet from the screen does not affect the worksheet saved on disk.

QUICK QUESTIONS

1. What is the main difference between the temporary and the permanent directory commands?
2. Should you give meaningful file extensions to your worksheets when you save them? Explain.
3. Write the command you would key to save a file called SHEET2 on your disk.
4. Does saving a worksheet clear your screen?
5. Write the command you would key to clear a worksheet from your screen.
6. What command do you use to exit from 1-2-3?

1. Key / **W**orksheet **E**rase **Y**es (**Y**es a second time if asked to verify the erasure).
2. At the end of your work session, key **/** **Q**uit **Y**es (**Y**es to verify if asked).

NEW COMMANDS AND KEYS

`'`. The label prefix character for left alignment.

`"`. The label prefix character for right alignment.

`^`. The label prefix character for center alignment.

/ Worksheet Column Set-Width. Narrows or widens a column.

/ File Directory *drive and path*. Sets a temporary directory for storing worksheet files.

/ Worksheet Global Default Directory *drive and path* Update Quit. Sets a permanent directory for storing worksheet files.

/ File Save. Saves a worksheet on disk.

/ Worksheet Erase Yes. Erases a worksheet from the screen.

FILES CREATED IN THIS LESSON

PRAC3
ACT31
ACT32
ACT33
CTPA

> ▶ **EXERCISE 3-7**
>
>
>
> Click on Worksheet, Erase, Yes (Yes a second time if asked to verify the erasure).

ACTIVITIES

Follow these steps to practice entering data into a worksheet.

ACTIVITY 3-1

1. If necessary, load 1-2-3 or clear the worksheet on your screen with / **Worksheet Erase Yes** (Yes if asked to verify).

2. Key the following main heading at [A1], allowing spillover: ALA CARTE MENU

3. Key the following column headings:
   [A3] [^] ITEMS
   [B3] ["] PRICE

4. Enter the following labels in Column A, beginning in cell A5:
   [A5] [^] Salad
   [A6] [^] Soup
   [A7] [^] Sandwich
   [A8] [^] Drink
   [A9] [^] Dessert

5. Widen column A to 12 characters. Press [/] **Worksheet Column Set-Width** [1] [2] [ENTER].

6. Enter the following numbers in column B, beginning in cell B5. (Insignificant zeros will not be displayed.)
   [B5] 2.25
   [B6] 1.80
   [B7] 2.50
   [B8] .75
   [B9] 1.25

7. Check the accuracy of the worksheet. Correct any errors.

8. Be sure you have set the directory for storing your files. Then save the worksheet on your disk with the file name ACT31 by keying / **File Save** ACT31 [ENTER].

9. Clear the worksheet by keying / **Worksheet Erase Yes** (Yes).

ACTIVITY 3-2

Follow these steps to practice entering data into a worksheet.

1. Enter a main heading in cell A1, spilling over into B1:
   [A1] MONTHLY EXPENSES

2. Key the following column headings:
   [A3] (^) BILL
   [B3] (^) COST
   [C3] (^) DATE DUE

3. Enter the following labels in Column A, beginning in cell A5:
   [A5] Rent
   [A6] Electric
   [A7] Water
   [A8] Telephone
   [A9] Food
   [A10] Car Payment
   [A11] Gas & Oil
   [A12] Leisure

4. Widen column A to 14 characters. Key (/) Worksheet Column Set-Width (1) (4) (ENTER).

5. Enter the following numbers in column B, beginning in cell B5:
   [B5] 310.00
   [B6] 48.65
   [B7] 15.43
   [B8] 34.76
   [B9] 195.28
   [B10] 165.55
   [B11] 62.00
   [B12] 78.88

6. Enter the following labels. Press the apostrophe label prefix character (') before each item that begins with a number. Begin the labels in cell C5:
   [C5] 15th
   [C6] 26th
   [C7] 15th
   [C8] 12th
   [C9] weekly
   [C10] 1st
   [C11] as needed
   [C12] weekly

7. Widen cell C to 11 characters.

8. Check the accuracy of the worksheet. Correct any errors.

9. Save the worksheet on your disk with the file name ACT32. Key / File Save ACT32 (ENTER).

10. Clear the worksheet with / Worksheet Erase Yes (Yes).

ACTIVITY 3-3

	A	B	C	D	E
1			CUSTOMER ACCOUNT BALANCES		
2					
3	ACCOUNT		ACCOUNT		
4	BALANCE		NUMBER	CUSTOMER NAME	
5					
6	45.22		456-22-8874	Williams, Richard Mrs.	
7	105.33		656-85-9114	Tipton, Gladys	
8	-22.5		551-34-2782	Mendez, Oscar	
9	3.66		461-82-4645	Richardson, Luetta Ms.	
10	557.25		405-86-3622	Anderson, Brett	
11	53.78		386-42-6890	Crowder, Tom	
12	69.42		312-86-2448	Isobe, Reiko	
13	245.36		865-44-9074	Tramplin, Belinda Mrs.	
14	15.99		566-28-7671	Johnson, Elliott Mrs.	
15	37.98		389-65-4430	Johnson, Robin	

Follow these steps to enter data into the worksheet shown above.

1. Begin the main heading in cell C1: CUSTOMER ACCOUNT BALANCES

2. Enter the column headings:
   [A3] ^ ACCOUNT
   [A4] ^ BALANCE
   [C3] ^ ACCOUNT
   [C4] ^ NUMBER
   [D4] ^ CUSTOMER NAME

3. Enter the numeric data in column A, beginning in cell A6.

4. Leave column B empty.

5. Enter the labels that begin with numbers in column C, beginning in cell C6.

6. Set the width of column C to 14 characters.

7. Enter the label data in column D, beginning in cell D6.

8. Set the width of column D to 23 characters.

9. Check the accuracy of the worksheet. Correct any errors.

10. Save the worksheet on your disk with the file name ACT33. Key / **File Save** ACT33 **ENTER**.

11. Clear the worksheet with / **Worksheet Erase Yes** (Yes) or exit 1-2-3 with / **Quit Yes** (Yes).

CRITICAL THINKING PROJECT 3

The scenario: You have been elected treasurer of the computer club at your school. One of the tasks of your office is to keep a record of each member's financial standing with the club. At this point, each member has paid $5 in club dues.

The project: First, think up a catchy but appropriate name for the club. Then create a 1-2-3 worksheet that includes main headings with the club name, the name of your school, and the current school year.

Include two column headings, one for the member names and one for the dues amounts. Key the members' names in column A; use the names of ten of your friends or classmates. In column B key the amount of dues paid by each member ($5). Somewhere on the worksheet include your name as treasurer. Save the worksheet as CTP3. Erase the worksheet from the screen.

LESSON 4

Retrieve and Print

OBJECTIVES
- Retrieve a worksheet
- Edit and replace a worksheet
- Print a worksheet

Estimated Time: 30 minutes

VOCABULARY
Anchor

Edit

Range

RETRIEVE A WORKSHEET

An existing worksheet is brought into main memory with the **File Retrieve** command. When you use this command, the third line of the control panel lists, in alphabetic order, the names of files with WK1 (1-2-3 Release 2.x) or WK3 (1-2-3 Release 3.x) file extensions. Select the desired file name, and then press Enter.

When your disk contains more files than 1-2-3 can display at once, press → to see other file names. If you prefer, you may instead key the name of the file you want to retrieve.

You may retrieve a worksheet while another worksheet is on your screen. Save the first worksheet if desired, because retrieving a new worksheet will erase the first worksheet from memory. *In Release 2.x, if you edit the first worksheet and do not save it before attempting to retrieve the new worksheet, 1-2-3 will prompt you:* **WORKSHEET CHANGES NOT SAVED! Retrieve the file anyway?** *Responding* **Yes** *erases the first file. Release 3.x does not give a warning; it simply erases the first worksheet.*

> **NOTE**
>
> To retrieve a file, key / **F**ile **R**etrieve. If your disk contains more worksheet files than 1-2-3 can display at once, press → to see more files.

> **NOTE**
>
> It is not necessary to erase a worksheet before retrieving another one, but the first worksheet will be erased from memory.

Retrieve the PRAC3 worksheet.

1. Key / **F**ile **R**etrieve.

2. Press → to move the pointer through the file list to PRAC3. Press **ENTER**.

The worksheet appears on your screen. Add the following data.

3. Move the worksheet pointer to cell A11 and key the following:

   [A11]   Mints
   [B11]   `'` 1 box
   [C11]   1.89

REPLACE A WORKSHEET

If you retrieve a worksheet, edit (change) it in some way, and save it a second time, you have the choice of giving the edited file a new name or the same name as the original file.

REPLACE A WORKSHEET WITH A NEW NAME

When you key / File Save, the original file name will appear on the second line of the control panel. If you wish to save the file with a new name, just key it.

Replace the PRAC3 worksheet with a new name, PRAC4A.

1. Key / **F**ile **S**ave

2. Key PRAC4A **ENTER** to give the worksheet a new name.

The worksheet is saved as PRAC4A, but it remains on your screen.

REPLACE A WORKSHEET WITH THE SAME NAME

When you key / File Save, the original file name will appear on the second line of the control panel. If you wish to save an edited file with the same name, press Enter after you key / File Save. Next you will be prompted to be sure you want to replace (erase) the original version with the edited version. As Figure 4-1 illustrates, the prompt gives the choices *Cancel*, *Replace*, and *Backup*.

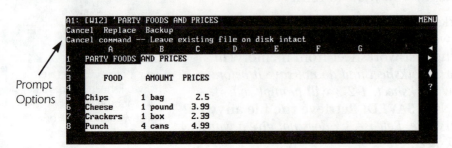

▶ **EXERCISE 4–1**

Click on File, Retrieve. Press → to move through the file list. When PRAC3 appears, click on it with the mouse button.

N O T E

When you saved an edited worksheet, you can give it a new name or keep the original one.

Figure 4-1
The Replace, Cancel, or Backup Options.

If you choose *Cancel*, the file is not saved (a 1-2-3 safety feature that helps to prevent accidental overwriting of the original disk file). If you choose *Replace*, the edited file is saved, overwriting the original file on the disk. The *Backup* option will give the disk file a BAK extension and save the edited version with the normal WK1 or WK3 extension.

Choose *Replace* to save a worksheet with its original name.

Be careful when you see the Replace option. Pressing Enter chooses **Cancel!**

QUICK QUESTIONS

1. What filenames do 1-2-3 display when you use the File Retrieve command? *Alphabetic*

2. In what order are filenames listed when you use the File Retrieve command? *Alphabetic Order*

3. When you retrieve a worksheet and edit it, what are your two choices when saving it?

    a.

    b.

4. What prompt do you see if you try to resave a file with the original file name?

After editing the PRAC4A file, you will resave it with the same name. First, change the price of the crackers to 2.99.

1. At cell C7, key 2.99 **ENTER**
2. Key / **F**ile **S**ave.
3. Press **ENTER** to accept the original file name.
4. Select **R**eplace.

The worksheet is saved on your disk as PRAC4A, but it remains on the screen. Erase the worksheet.

5. Key / **W**orksheet **E**rase **Y**es.

▶ **EXERCISE 4–3**

Do additonal practice with retrieve, edit and resave.

1. Retrieve the PRAC4A worksheet.
2. Key / **F**ile **R**etrieve PRAC4A **ENTER**.

Save the worksheet with a new name, PRAC4B.

3. Key / **F**ile **S**ave.
4. Key PRAC4B.
5. Press **ENTER** when you are sure you have spelled the file name correctly.

▶ **EXERCISE 4–4**

The quickest way to retrieve a worksheet is to key its filename. It is not necessary to key the file extension.

LESSON 4 RETRIEVE AND PRINT

Erase the worksheet.

6. Key / **W**orksheet **E**rase **Y**es.

PRINT

To print a basic worksheet on the printer, use the **Print** command (outlined in Figure 4-2). Before you begin the print command, be sure your name and any other identification is on the worksheet and check that the printer is ready. Go to cell A1 and then begin the print command (steps 3 and 4 in Figure 4-2).

When setting the print range (step 5 in Figure 4-2), press period (.) at cell A1 to anchor it as the beginning of the range. Once you anchor the beginning of the range, the worksheet is highlighted as you move toward the end of the range. The end of the range is the cell that is the *last row and last column used in the current worksheet.* Cursor to the end of the range and press Enter.

The final steps tell 1-2-3 to begin a new page with Align, start printing with Go, eject the paper in the printer with Page, and end the print menu with Quit. You do not have to wait for printing to end before continuing your work.

N O T E

It is not necessary to clear a worksheet from the screen before retrieving a different one.

BASIC PRINTING

1.	Position the paper in the printer.	Sets the top of form.
2.	Press **HOME**	Moves the pointer to cell A1, the beginning of the print range.
3.	/ **P**rint	Begins the Print command.
4.	**P**rinter	Prints the file to the printer.
5.	**R**ange **Highlight the range of cells** Press Enter	Allows you to set the range of cells to be printed.
6.	**A**lign	Resets the page number to 1 and tells 1-2-3 it is beginning to print at the top of a page.
7.	**G**o	Begins printing.
8.	**P**age	Advances paper in the printer for the completed document.
9.	**Q**uit	Exits the Print menu and returns to Ready mode.

Figure 4-2.
Steps to print a worksheet.

QUICK QUESTIONS

1. What is the first step in the basic printing of a worksheet according to Figure 4.2?
2. Why should you press HOME before using the Print command?
3. What key do you press to anchor the beginning of a print range?
4. What cell should you designate as the end of a print range?
5. What key do you press to show the end of a range?
6. What is the purpose of Align when using the Print command?
7. Why is it important to use the Page option of the Print command?
8. What option do you choose to exit from the Print menu?

Follow the steps below and those listed in Figure 4-2 to print the PRAC4B worksheet.

EXERCISE 4–5

1. Retrieve the PRAC4B worksheet.

Next, key the information you and your instructor need to identify your printed worksheets, such as your name and the name of the worksheet. Always leave one blank row between the worksheet data and your identification line. Key the identification as one label, spilling over into the cells at the right.

2. Write the identifying information your instructor wants you to key on every worksheet, and then key it in the PRAC4B worksheet beginning at cell A13.

3. Check the paper in the printer and set the top of a new sheet if necessary.

Click on Print, Printer, Range.

4. Key HOME to move the pointer to cell A1, the beginning of the print range.

5. Key / **P**rint **P**rinter **R**ange.

If you are using the keyboard, the next instruction will anchor cell A1 as the beginning of the print range; it will highlight the entire range if you are using the mouse. (If necessary to reset the beginning of the range, press ESC before anchoring.)

Point to cell A1 and then hold down the mouse button as you drag the mouse down to row 11 and across to column C, highlighting the entire print range. Release the mouse button when you reach cell C11. (See Figure 4-3.)

6. [A1] **.**

Move the pointer to the end of the print range.

7. Key ⬇ to move to A13, the bottom row of the range, and then key ➡ to move to cell C13, the last column and row of the print range (or farther). See Figure 4-3. (If the line with your identifying information extends beyond column C, you will have to extend your print range.)

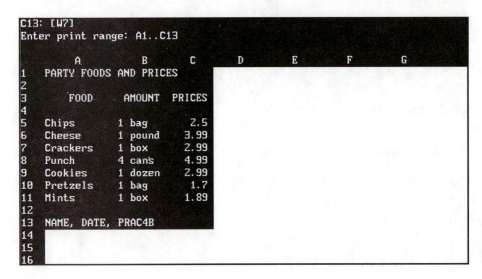

Figure 4-3
Highlighting the print range.

The range is highlighted as you move toward the end of the range; press Enter to show the end of it.

8. [C13] **ENTER** to end the range.

Continue the print command. The print menu is shown in Figure 4-4.

At cell C13, click the mouse button to end the range.

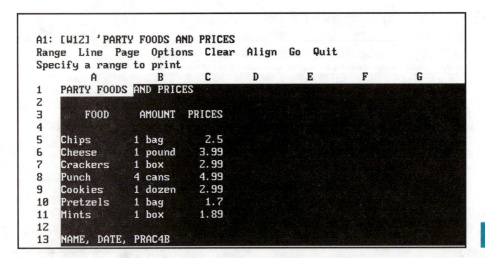

Figure 4-4
The Print Menu.

9. Key **A**lign to clear for printing a new page.
10. Key **G**o to begin printing.

Click on Align.

Click on Go.

46 LESSON 4 RETRIEVE AND PRINT

11. Key **P**age to eject the paper in the printer. (Printing does not have to be completed.)
12. Key **Q**uit to exit the print menu and return to Ready mode.
13. Save the worksheet on your disk, replacing the original version. The print range you set will remain with the worksheet on disk to facilitate future printing.
14. If your work session is over, quit 1-2-3. Otherwise, go on to Activity 4-1. It is not necessary to erase the worksheet before retrieving a new one.

Click on **P**age to eject the paper in the printer.

Click on **Q**uit to exit the print menu and return to Ready mode.

The Print Page command ejects the worksheet in the printer.

NEW COMMANDS AND KEYS

/ File Retrieve. Retrieves a worksheet file from disk.

/ File Save Replace. Replaces a worksheet on disk with the edited version on the screen.

/ File Save Cancel. Cancels the saving of the worksheet on the screen.

/ File Save Backup. Renames the original worksheet on disk with a BAK file extension and saves the worksheet on the screen with the original name, including a WK1 (Release 2.x) or WK3 (Release 3.x) file extension.

/ File Print Printer Range Align Go Page Quit. Prints a basic worksheet.

FILES CREATED IN THIS LESSON

PRAC4A

PRAC4B

ACTIVITIES

ACTIVITY 4-1

1. Load 1-2-3 if necessary. Retrieve the ACT31 worksheet.
2. Key your personal identification line, including the file name ACT31.
3. Print the worksheet. Be careful to include your identification line in the range.
4. Save the file on your disk, choosing Replace.

ACTIVITY 4-2

1. Retrieve the ACT32 worksheet.
2. Key your personal identification line, including the file name ACT32.
3. Print the worksheet. Be careful to include your identification line in the range.
4. Save the file on your disk, choosing Replace.

ACTIVITY 4-3

1. Retrieve the ACT33 worksheet.
2. Key your personal identification line, including the file name ACT33.
3. Print the worksheet. Be careful to include your identification line in the range.
4. Save the file on your disk, choosing Replace.
5. Quit 1-2-3 or go on to the next section.

LESSON 5

Formulas

OBJECTIVES

- Use numeric symbols
- Recognize a numeric cell that is too narrow
- Construct formulas using numbers and cell values
- Point to cells
- Correct cell contents with the Edit feature

Estimated Time: 30 minutes.

VOCABULARY

Edit mode
Formula
Overstrike
Point to cells
Scientific notation

USING NUMBERS AND NUMERIC SYMBOLS

As you learned in Lesson 3, when you key a numeric digit or numeric symbol as the first character of a cell, 1-2-3 assumes you are entering a number or formula and will display *Value* on the mode indicator. Only values can be used in calculations.

Numeric symbols include the plus sign, minus sign, decimal point, and parenthesis. (Keying a number surrounded with parentheses has the same effect as preceding the number with a plus sign.) Never use a label prefix character for a value.

NOTE

Only values can be used in calculations.

EXERCISE 5-1

1. Load 1-2-3 if necessary.

Watch the mode indicator as you key several numbers with numeric symbols. Notice which numeric symbols appear in the worksheet cell when the entry is complete.

2. Key the following:

    [A1] 12345

    [A2] .5531

    [A3] +3792

    [A4] -8888

    [A5] (2706)

    [A6] 37.00

Did you notice that only decimal points followed by significant numbers and minus signs for negative numbers are the only numeric symbols that appear in the cell? You should also note that numbers automatically align on the right of the cell. Compare your worksheet with Figure 5-1.

> **NOTE**
> A number must align on the right of the cell with no label prefix character.

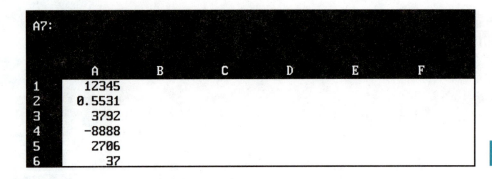

Figure 5-1
Worksheet Check.

SPECIAL CHARACTERS

You should not key *commas, spaces,* or *dollar signs* with a number that will be calculated. 1-2-3 will either beep at you and put you in Edit mode to correct the entry (Release 2.x) **or enter the number without the commas, spaces, or dollar signs (Rel. 3.x).**

A NUMERIC CELL THAT IS TOO NARROW

If a number or the result of a formula exceeds the width of a cell, asterisks (*) will appear across the cell, or the number will be converted to scientific notation (for example, 3.4E+09, which is the number 3,400,000,000). To correct this problem when it happens, widen the cell so the number can be shown in its entirety.

> **NOTE**
> Scientific notation or asterisks warn that a numeric cell is too narrow.

52 LESSON 5 FORMULAS

QUICK QUESTIONS

1. What must be displayed on the mode indicator as you key a cell entry that will be used in a calculation?
2. Would the entry "3776 be calculated? Why or why not?
3. If you press a plus or minus sign as the first character of a cell, what type of entry have you created?
4. Which two numeric symbols will appear in a worksheet cell?
5. Do numbers align at the right or the left of a cell?
6. Why may 1-2-3 beep at you if you key *66, 540, 282*?
7. What should you do if a number is changed to scientific notation or asterisks?

Key a number with incorrect special characters. 1-2-3 Release 2.x will beep and not accept the number until it is edited, but Release 3.x will accept the entry (although it will not display the commas). **(Release 2.x only: Now use the (←) cursor key to position the cursor on one of the commas. Press (DELETE). Delete the second comma and then press (ENTER). The number is now acceptable without the commas.)**

1. [A1] 2,376,127 (ENTER).

Key a number that exceeds the column width.

2. Use the Goto feature to go to cell C1.
3. [C1] 3447692364 (ENTER).

The number is displayed in scientific notation or asterisks because the cell has the default width of nine characters, and the number contains ten digits. Widen cell C1 so the number can be shown in its entirety.

4. [C1] (/) **W**orksheet **C**olumn **S**et-Width.
5. Press (→) until the column is wide enough to display the value.
6. Press (ENTER).

Having to widen columns for both labels and numbers is a common occurrence.

7. Erase the worksheet from the screen without saving it. When prompted for verification, key (y) for **Y**es.

FORMULAS

Formulas perform calculations on numbers, on other formulas, or on the contents of other numeric cells. You may want to review the *How 1-2-3 Calculates* section in Lesson 1 before using formulas in this section. The following are examples of formulas:

1376.50*375

(4627)-(50*.376)

+D5/D1

+B3-(B4*.7)

+C12+E8

When you enter a formula, 1-2-3 displays the *result* of the formula in the worksheet cell. You can view the formula itself by looking at the contents line on the control panel. (See Figure 5-2.)

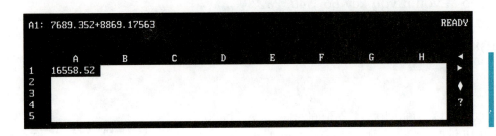

Figure 5-2
1-2-3 displays the formula on the contents line and the result of the formula in the cell.

CALCULATING WITH NUMBERS

The basic operators are: + for addition, - for subtraction, * for multiplication, and / for division. Do NOT space anywhere within a formula. You may use the numbers on the numeric keypad or the numbers on the top row of the alphanumeric keyboard to key a formula.

Start with a clear worksheet. Use the numeric keypad or the numbers on the top row of the alphanumeric keyboard to key numbers and operators. DO NOT place **spaces** anywhere in the formulas.

▶ **EXERCISE 5-3**

1. Widen column A to 15.
2. [A1] 7689.352+8869.17563 **ENTER**.
3. Note that cell A1 displays the result of the formula. The contents line, however, displays the formula itself. What is the result of the formula?
4. [A3] 3766.917-211.27 **ENTER**. What is the result of the formula?
5. [A5] 476.175*7843.68 **ENTER**. What is the result?
6. [A7] 4289.75/874.18 **ENTER**. What is the result?
7. Widen column C to 15.
8. [C2] 4781.44+(576.44*1.12) **ENTER**.

Keep the worksheet on your screen.

CALCULATING WITH CELL VALUES

When using cell values in a formula, move the pointer to each cell as you build the formula. This is called **pointing** to cells, and it is more accurate than keying cell addresses yourself. Begin the formula with + in the cell in which the result should appear.

For example, to get the result of the formula A5-C2 in cell C4, follow these steps: key + in C4, point to cell A5, key (−), point to cell C2, and press Enter.

Pointing to cells is more accurate than keying cell addresses.

Begin a formula with + in the cell in which the result should appear.

QUICK QUESTIONS

1. What three types of values may be used in formulas?
   a.
   b.
   c.
2. Where will an actual formula be displayed?
3. Where will the result of a formula be displayed?
4. Write the operators used for addition, subtraction, multiplication, and division.
5. Where, if at all, can you place spaces within a formula?
6. When building a formula by pointing to cells, where should you begin the formula and what should you key there?

► EXERCISE 5-4

Using the worksheet from Exercise 5-3, subtract the value at C2 from the value at A5 by pointing to cells. Begin by pressing + in the cell where the answer should appear (C4).

1. [C4] (+)
2. Move the pointer to A5.

Notice the cell contents line on the control panel as you build the formula. Next, key the appropriate arithmetic operator for subtraction.

3. [A5] (−)
4. Move the pointer to C2, the last cell in the formula. Press (**ENTER**).
5. Look at the cell contents for the formula you have built. What is the formula?
6. Look at the worksheet cell for the result of the formula. What is the result?

LESSON 5 FORMULAS 55

7. Build another formula, A1 divided by A3 minus A7, with the result in cell C6:

    [C6] [+]

    Point to A1.

    Press [/]

    Point to A3.

    Press [−]

    Point to A7.

    Press [ENTER] to complete the formula. What is the formula at C6?

8. Next, find the total of the numbers in column A:

    [A9] [+]

    Point to A7. Press [+]

    Point to A5. Press [+]

    Point to A3. Press [+]

    Point to A1. Press [ENTER] to complete the formula.

9. The result appears at A9, where the original plus sign was keyed. What is the result?

10. Total all the numbers in column C using similar steps to those above. The result of the formula should appear at cell C8. What is the result?

11. Check your work with Figure 5-3.

Save the worksheet as PRAC5A. Leave it on your screen for the next exercise.

```
C18: [W15]

           A            B            C            D            E
 1    16558.52763
 2                                 5427.0528
 3        3555.647
 4                               3729537.2712
 5    3734964.324
 6                              -0.2502040234
 7    4.907170148
 8                               3734964.0738
 9    3755083.4058
10
```

Figure 5-3
Worksheet Check for PRAC5A.

EDIT CELLS

Take a few moments to review how to correct miskeyed data according to the Error Correction Chart in Lesson 3. When currently keying incorrect data in a cell, you should backspace to erase and then rekey; but when you have moved on to another cell, use the **Edit** feature to correct errors.

To use the Edit feature, move to the cell that contains the error. Press F2 to display the cell contents on the control panel's edit line. Then use the cursor keys to move to the inaccurate character(s) and **overstrike**, **delete**, or **add** (insert) new characters. The default action in Edit mode is to add new characters. End the Edit mode by pressing Enter.

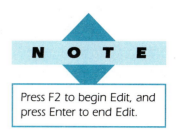

Press F2 to begin Edit, and press Enter to end Edit.

OVERSTRIKE

Press the Insert key to begin and end the overstrike action when in Edit mode. *OVR* will appear on the status line to verify overstrike of characters.

Use overstrike to edit several cells.

EXERCISE 5-5

1. Move the pointer to cell A5. At A5, press **F2** to edit the cell. The cell contents appear on the edit line, the second line on the control panel, as you can see in Figure 5-4. Use the edit line to edit the cell.

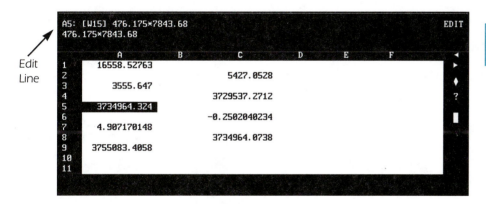

Figure 5-4
Edit the cell contents using the edit line.

2. Press ← to place the cursor on the **1** in the first number on the edit line. Press **INSERT** to overstrike. Press **2** as the correct number.

3. Press → to place the cursor on the **3** in the second number. You are still in overstrike mode, so just press **9**.

4. Check the formula: 476.275*7849.68. Once you have the formula corrected, press **ENTER** with the cursor at any position. The **OVR** message will disappear from the status line as you are returned to the default action (insert).

Edit another cell. Make the formula at cell A7 a subtraction formula instead of division. Also, add an additional subtraction of 379.228 at the end of the formula.

5. Move the pointer to cell A7.

6. Press **F2** to begin the Edit feature.

7. Move the cursor to the division sign (/) and press **INSERT** to overstrike. Key the minus sign (–). Press **INSERT** again to end overstrike.
8. Move to the right end of the formula using the **END** key.
9. Key **–** 379.228 **ENTER**.
10. Look at cell A7. What is the result of the new formula?

ADD CHARACTERS

To add (insert) characters within a cell when using the Edit feature, simply key the characters.

Edit a cell by adding (inserting) characters.

▶ **EXERCISE 5–6**

1. Goto cell C4 and press **F2** to Edit.
2. Press **←** to move to the minus sign (-).
3. Key **+** **A** **7**.
4. The new formula should be +A5+A7-C2. Press **ENTER** when the formula is correct.

DELETE CHARACTERS

To delete characters when you are working in the Edit mode, press the Delete key.

Edit a cell with Delete.

▶ **EXERCISE 5–7**

1. Goto cell C2. Press **F2** to Edit.
2. Press **HOME** to move to the far left of the contents, on the first **4** of 4781.44.
3. Key **DELETE** to erase 4781.44+.
4. The new formula is (576.44*1.12). Press **ENTER** when you are finished correcting the formula.
5. Save the worksheet as PRAC5B and then erase the worksheet.

QUICK QUESTIONS

1. How should you correct an error when you are still keying in the cell?
2. How should you correct an error when you have moved on to another cell?
3. Which key do you use to activate Edit?
4. What three actions can you perform when editing?
   a.
   b.
   c.
5. How do you end the Edit feature?
6. What key do you press to overstrike characters in Edit mode?
7. How can you add characters to a cell in Edit?
8. What key do you press to delete characters in Edit mode?

NEW COMMANDS AND KEYS

[+]. The formula operator for addition.

[−]. The formula operator for subtraction.

[*]. The formula operator for multiplication.

[/]. The formula operator for additon.

[F2]. The Edit feature. It allows you to edit the contents of a cell.

[INSERT]. Used to strikeover characters when in Edit mode.

[DELETE]. Used to erase characters when in Edit mode.

FILES CREATED OR EDITED IN THIS SECTION

PRAC5A

PRAC5B

ACT51

ACT52

ACT53

ACTIVITIES

(Template File: ACT51TP)

ACTIVITY 5-1

	A	B	C	D
1	42.85	576.15		
2	7733.24	99.08		
3	963.71	374.79		
4	66.22	53.47		
5	17.8	69.07		
6	59.35	0.37		
7	68.55	37.89		
8	967.43	6.32		
9	80.96	9715.63		
10				

(If template files are available, you can retrieve the ACT51TP worksheet instead of keying the data in Step 1.)

1. On a clean worksheet, use the numeric keypad to key the figures in the worksheet above. Check for accuracy; edit as needed.

2. Key formulas that will calculate the following addition and subtraction at the designated cells. Point to cells rather than key the cell addresses. Begin each formula with a plus. Write the formulas in the spaces provided below.

    [C1] The sum of A1 and B1

    [C2] The sum of A2 and B2

    [C3] The difference between A3 and B3

    [C4] The sum of A1 and B4

    [C5] The sum of A7, A8, and A9

    [C6] The difference between B1 and A7

3. Save the worksheet as ACT51 and then use it for the following activity.

ACTIVITY 5-2

1. Retrieve the ACT51 worksheet completed in the previous activity to complete the following tasks.

2. Key formulas that will calculate the following multiplication and division operations at the designated cells. Point to cells rather than key the cell addresses. Begin each formula with a plus. Write the formulas in the spaces provided below.

   [D1] Divide B5 by A5.

   [D2] Divide A6 by B6.

   [D3] Multiply B7 by B6.

   [D4] Multiply A8 by B8.

   [D5] Multiply A4 by A5 by B7.

   [D6] Multiply A9 by B7 and then subtract the product from B9.

3. Save the worksheet as ACT52 and then print it.

4. Erase the worksheet.

(Template file: ACT53TP)

ACTIVITY 5-3

```
                    A                   B       C       D
 1      ACTION CRANES, INC.
 2      INCOME STATEMENT
 3      FOR QUARTER ENDED DECEMBER 31, 19—
 4
 5      Revenue
 6         Net Sales                127367
 7         Cost of Sales             11866
 8            Gross Profit            xxxx
 9            Miscellaneous Income    1306
10              Total Income          xxxx
11
12      Expenses
13         Advertising                8575
14         Utilities                  1200
15         Supplies                    328
16         Salaries                   8500
17         Transportation             2690
18            Total Expenses          xxxx
19
20      Net Profit Before Taxes       xxxx
21
22      Taxes                         xxxx
23
24      Net Profit After Taxes        xxxx
25
```

(If template files are available, you can retrieve the ACT53TP worksheet instead of keying steps 1 and 2.)

1. On a clean worksheet, complete the following steps to key the income statement shown above. Check for accuracy; edit as needed.

2. First, key the heading labels and the labels in column A. Because 1-2-3 does not recognize the Tab key, you must use the spacebar to indent labels. Press the spacebar 2, 4, or 6 times as shown before keying the labels that are indented. After you key column A, widen it for the longest line in the column; do not consider the main headings.

3. Key formulas that will calculate the following amounts at the cells where the Xs appear. (Xs do not appear on the template file.) Point to cells rather than key the cell addresses. Begin each formula with a plus. Write the cell formulas in the spaces provided below.

   Gross Profit = Net Sales - Cost of Sales

   Total Income = Gross Profit + Miscellaneous Income

   Total Expenses = Sum of all expenses

   Net Profit Before Taxes = Total Income - Total Expenses

   Taxes = .16 * Net Profit Before Taxes

   Net Profit After Taxes = Net Profit Before Taxes - Taxes

4. Save the worksheet as ACT53 and then print it.

CRITICAL THINKING PROJECT 5

If necessary, retrieve the ACT53 worksheet. Complete the following "what if" activities on the worksheet.

Before changing data for each "what if" activity, record the contents of the cell before the change so you can return to the original value after playing "what if." Use the Edit feature when appropriate. After altering a cell's contents to see its effect on the worksheet, record your answer, and then **return the cell to its previous contents**. Do NOT save any changes to the worksheet. If necessary, erase the worksheet and retrieve ACT53 again.

The first activity has been done as an example; work through it to be sure you understand the process for completing the following tasks.

1. Record the original contents of the cell for the Salaries amount now (B16) _8500_. What will the Net Profit After Taxes be if Salaries are doubled? (At cell B16, press F2 to edit, and then add *2 to the figure, resulting in the formula **8500*2**, which doubles the Salaries amount. Next, look at the new Net Profit After Taxes amount at cell B24. Write the new figure on the line.) _73091.76._ (Now, return the Salaries amount to the original figure. Go to cell B16, press F2 to edit, and delete the *2, returning the cell contents to the original 8500.)

2. Record the original contents of the cell for the Miscellaneous Income amount now (B9). _____ What will Total Income be if there is no Miscellaneous Income? _____ What will Net Profit Before Taxes be if there is no Miscellaneous Income? _____

3. The initial tax rate is 16% (.16). What will the Net Profit After Taxes be if Taxes are increased to 18.5%? _____

4. Record the original Net Sales amount now. _____. What will the Total Income be if Net Sales are increased by 30%? _____ What will the Net Profit Before Taxes be if Net Sales are increased by 30%? What will the Taxes be if Net Sales are increased by 30%? _____

5. Record the original Net Sales amount now. _____. What would Net Sales have to be for Net Profit After Taxes to be $120000.7? _____

6. Would it be beneficial if the company hired an additional employee at a salary of $4300 for the quarter, if Net Sales would increase by $5300 and Cost of Sales would increase by only $250? _____

   Explain your answer. _____
   _____
   _____

64 LESSON 5 FORMULAS

LESSON 6

Functions

OBJECTIVES

- Identify the parts of a function
- Point to function arguments
- Use @sum, @avg, @min, and @max functions
- Use @count and @repeat functions

Estimated Time: 45 minutes

VOCABULARY

Argument

Character string

Function

Function name

Scroll

1-2-3 provides built-in shortcuts, called **functions**, for complex formulas and other types of operations. There are many functions available for mathematical, statistical, financial, and logical operations, among others. You will use just a few of them.

Because functions must be preceded with the @ sign, they are often called @functions or "at functions." The following are examples of the types of @functions you will use in this book:

@SUM(D5.G5)
@AVG(B2.B12)
@MIN(E5.J5)
@MAX(C3.C22)
@COUNT(A5.A22)
@REPEAT("#",22)

CONSTRUCTING A FUNCTION

A function is made up of three parts. The first part is the @ sign, which is created by holding Shift while pressing the 2 key. The next part is the **function name**, (for example, SUM for add, AVG for average, MIN for minimum, and MAX for maximum).

The third part of some functions, like the ones shown on page 65, requires an argument. An **argument**, enclosed in parentheses, often lists the data on which the function is to be performed. Many arguments are a range of cells. For example, the function @SUM(D5.G5) contains the argument (D5.G5). This function will add the range of cells from D5 through G5.

When keying a function for a range of cells, press [.] only once in the middle of the argument, even though 1-2-3 will display two periods on the control panel. Do not key any spaces within the function. Press F1 for Help about a function while you are keying it.

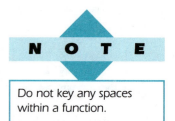

Do not key any spaces within a function.

@SUM FUNCTION

The @SUM function adds the contents of a range of cells. As you can see in Figure 6-1, column A of the ACT33 worksheet contains the account balances of customers. To find the total of column A, you add all the account balances in cells A6 through A15. The following formula would total those cells: + A6 + A7 + A8 + A9 + A10 + A11 + A12 + A13 + A14 + A15. However, a much simpler way to add the group of adjacent cells is by using the @sum function, with the list of cells to add (A6 through A15) as the argument. The function would be @SUM(A6.A15).

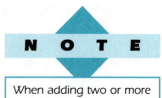

When adding two or more adjacent cells, use the @SUM function.

```
E20:

              A           B           C                    D                E
1                                  CUSTOMER ACCOUNT BALANCES
2
3         ACCOUNT                ACCOUNT
4         BALANCE                NUMBER         CUSTOMER NAME
5
6           45.22                456-22-8874    Williams, Richard Mrs.
7          105.33                656-85-9114    Tipton, Gladys
8          -22.5                 551-34-2782    Mendez, Oscar
9            3.66                461-82-4645    Richardson, Luetta Ms.
10         557.25                405-86-3622    Anderson, Brett
11          53.78                386-42-6890    Crowder, Tom
12          69.42                312-86-2448    Isobe, Reiko
13         245.36                865-44-9074    Tramplin, Belinda Mrs.
14          15.99                566-28-7671    Johnson, Elliott Mrs.
15          37.98                389-65-4430    Johnson, Robin
16
```

Figure 6-1
The ACT33 worksheet.

Use the @SUM function to add a series of cells.

EXERCISE 6-1

1. Load 1-2-3 if necessary.
2. Retrieve the ACT33 worksheet.
3. Goto cell A17.

If cell A17 already contains data, do not worry. The new contents of the cell will automatically overwrite the previous contents of the cell.

4. [A17] @sum(a6.a15) **(ENTER)**

The **result** of the function appears in cell A17. The function itself appears in the control panel on the cell contents line.

NOTE

It is not necessary to erase the contents of a cell before placing new data in the cell. New data will automatically overwrite the previous data.

Identify the value at A17 by keying a descriptive label in cell B17.

5. [B17] TOTAL **(ENTER)**
6. Key the data below to be calculated with an @sum function. As the worksheet gets larger, the screen may move, or **scroll**, as you move the pointer.

   [E3] PREVIOUS
   [E4] BALANCE
   [E6] 55.86
   [E7] 34.40
   [E8] 12.50
   [E9] 3.66
   [E10] 450.32
   [E11] 53.78

   [E12] 112.65
   [E13] 371.55
   [E14] 68.99
   [E15] 37.98

NOTE

In a large document, the display often moves, or **scrolls**, as you work.

Since pointing to cells is more accurate than keying cell addresses, always point to a function argument. Move the pointer up or down, left or right, whichever is most convenient. When pointing to the argument, press period (.) to anchor the beginning of the range. After keying the ending parenthesis, press Enter to end the argument range. To use a mouse, simply click and drag to highlight the argument; press the ending parenthesis, and then press Enter to end the argument.

NOTE

Pointing to cells is more accurate than keying cell addresses.

LESSON 6 FUNCTIONS 67

QUICK QUESTIONS

1. What is the name for the 1-2-3 built-in shortcuts for formulas and other operations?
2. List the three parts of a function.
   a.
   b.
   c.
3. What is an argument?
4. Write the function that would add cells B3 through B8.
5. After keying, where should you look to see the result of a function?
6. After keying, where should you look to see the actual function used in a cell?
7. What should you key to identify the result of a formula or function?
8. What term refers to the movement of the screen when you work on larger worksheets?
9. Why is it better to point to cells rather than key the cell addresses?
10. What is the purpose of the period when designating a range of cells for an argument?

EXERCISE 6-2

Construct a function by pointing to cells.

1. [E17] @sum (**(**)
2. Press (**↑**) until the pointer is on cell E15. (Look at the contents line.)

The period is used as an **anchor** to establish the beginning of the range of cells to be added.

3. Key (**.**) to anchor E15 as the beginning of the range.
4. Press (**↑**) to point to cell E6.
5. [E6] (**)**) **ENTER**

Look at the contents line. It should display: @sum(E15..E6). If it is not correct, repeat the steps beginning at E17.

6. [D17] (**"**) TOTAL

Check your work against Figure 6-2. Keep the worksheet on your screen.

Click on cell E15 and drag the mouse pointer to cell E6. Release the mouse button.

N O T E

Use the period to **anchor** the beginning of a range of cells in a function argument.

Key (**)**) and **ENTER**.

Figure 6-2
Worksheet Check after using the @SUM function.

```
A19:                                                              READY
        A            B           C              D              E
 1                         CUSTOMER ACCOUNT BALANCES
 2
 3    ACCOUNT                ACCOUNT                         PREVIOUS
 4    BALANCE                NUMBER       CUSTOMER NAME      BALANCE
 5
 6      45.22             456-22-8874    Williams, Richard Mrs.   55.86
 7     105.33             656-85-9114    Tipton, Gladys           34.4
 8     -22.5              551-34-2782    Mendez, Oscar            12.5
 9       3.66             461-82-4645    Richardson, Luetta Ms.    3.66
10     557.25             405-86-3622    Anderson, Brett         450.32
11      53.78             386-42-6890    Crowder, Tom             53.78
12      69.42             312-86-2448    Isobe, Reiko            112.65
13     245.36             865-44-9074    Tramplin, Belinda Mrs.  371.55
14      15.99             566-28-7671    Johnson, Elliott Mrs.    68.99
15      37.98             389-65-4430    Johnson, Robin           37.98
16
17    1111.49 TOTAL                                   TOTAL    1201.69
```

@AVG FUNCTION

This function calculates the average of a list of values. The average function totals a set of values and then divides the total by the number of values.

NOTE
@AVG calculates the average of a list of values.

▶ **EXERCISE 6-3**

Find the average account balance.

1. Goto A18.
2. [A18] @avg (
3. Point to A15. Key . to anchor A15 as the beginning of the function range.
4. Point to A6. Key) **ENTER** to show the end of the function range.
5. [B18] AVERAGE **ENTER**

Find the average previous balance.

6. [E18] @avg (
7. Point to E15. Key . to anchor E15 as the beginning of the function range.
8. Point to E6. Key) **ENTER** to show the end of the function range.
9. [D18] " AVERAGE **ENTER**

@MIN FUNCTION

The @MIN function displays the smallest, or *minimum*, value in a group of cells.

NOTE
@MIN displays the smallest value in a group of cells.

LESSON 6 FUNCTIONS

> **EXERCISE 6-4**

Find the minimum current account balance.

1. [A19] @min **(**
2. Point to A15. Key **.** to anchor A15 as the beginning of the function range.
3. Point to A6. Key **)** **ENTER** to show the end of the function range.
4. [B19] MINIMUM **ENTER**

Find the minimum previous balance.

5. [E19] @min **(**
6. Point to E15. Key **.** to anchor E15 as the beginning of the function range.
7. Point to E6. Key **)** **ENTER** to show the end of the function range.
8. [D19] **"** MINIMUM **ENTER**

@MAX FUNCTION

The @MAX function displays the largest, or *maximum*, value in a group of cells.

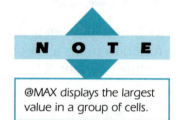

NOTE

@MAX displays the largest value in a group of cells.

Find the maximum current account balance.

> **EXERCISE 6-5**

1. [A20] @max **(**
2. Point to A15. Key **.** to anchor A15 as the beginning of the function range.
3. Point to A6. Key **)** **ENTER** to show the end of the function range.
4. [B20] MAXIMUM

Find the maximum previous balance.

5. [E20] @max **(**
6. Point to E15. Key **.**
7. Point to E6. Key **)** **ENTER** .
8. [D20] **"** MAXIMUM **ENTER**
9. Compare your completed worksheet with Figure 6-3.
10. Save your worksheet as PRAC6A. You will use it for the next exercise.

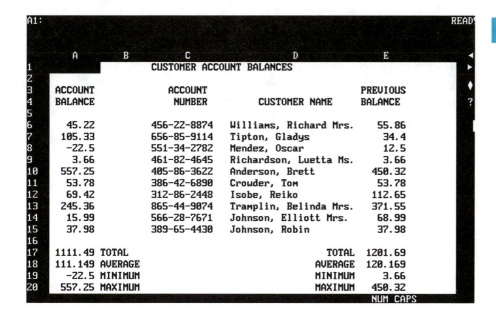

Figure 6-3
The PRAC6A Worksheet.

QUICK QUESTIONS

1. Write a function that averages cells D2 through D9.

2. Write a function that finds the smallest value in cells D5 through D12.

3. Write a function that finds the largest value in cells A6 through A12.

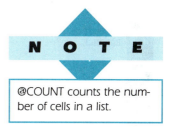

@COUNT counts the number of cells in a list.

@COUNT

This function is used to count the number of cells in a list of cells. This function is very helpful if you have a long list.

1. Retrieve the PRAC6A worksheet (if it is not already on your screen).

Count the number of customers. To do this, use the @count function to count the number of customers in cells D6 through D15. Place the solution in cell E21.

2. [E21] @count `(`

3. Point to cell D15. Key `.`.

4. Point to cell D6. Key `)` `ENTER`.

Key a label for the new figure.

5. [D21] Number of Customers `ENTER`

@REPEAT

The @REPEAT function repeats a character or **character string** (a group of characters) a specified number of times. The argument for the @REPEAT function is ("characters",number of repeats). The characters can be one or more characters on the keyboard, and the number of repeats can be any number you desire. A comma separates the characters and the number of repeats in the function statement.

NOTE

@REPEAT repeats a character string.

▶ **EXERCISE 6-7**

We will "dress up" the PRAC6A worksheet by placing equal signs (=) in the blank rows.

1. [A2] @repeat ("=",63) **ENTER**
2. [A5] @repeat ("=",63) **ENTER**
3. On your own, key the same @REPEAT function at cell A16.

Now remove the equal signs in row 5. This can be done easily by telling 1-2-3 to repeat a series of spaces instead of equal signs. When you key the @REPEAT function below, place a space between the quote marks.

4. [A5] @repeat(" ",63) **ENTER**
5. Check your worksheet against Figure 6-4.
6. Save your worksheet as PRAC6B. Erase the worksheet.

```
A1:                                                              READY

         A       B         C              D            E
                        CUSTOMER ACCOUNT BALANCES
 1
 2  ===============================================================
 3  ACCOUNT           ACCOUNT                        PREVIOUS
 4  BALANCE           NUMBER         CUSTOMER NAME   BALANCE
 5
 6     45.22          456-22-8874    Williams, Richard Mrs.    55.86
 7    105.33          656-85-9114    Tipton, Gladys            34.4
 8    -22.5           551-34-2782    Mendez, Oscar             12.5
 9      3.66          461-82-4645    Richardson, Luetta Ms.     3.66
10    557.25          405-86-3622    Anderson, Brett          450.32
11     53.78          386-42-6890    Crowder, Tom              53.78
12     69.42          312-86-2448    Isobe, Reiko             112.65
13    245.36          865-44-9074    Tramplin, Belinda Mrs.   371.55
14     15.99          566-28-7671    Johnson, Elliott Mrs.     68.99
15     37.98          389-65-4430    Johnson, Robin            37.98
16  ===============================================================
17   1111.49 TOTAL                           TOTAL            1201.69
18    111.149 AVERAGE                        AVERAGE           120.169
19    -22.5 MINIMUM                          MINIMUM             3.66
20    557.25 MAXIMUM                         MAXIMUM           450.32
                                                                  NUM
```

Figure 6-4
The PRAC6B Worksheet.

QUICK QUESTIONS

1. Write a function that counts the number of cells in A6 through A22.
2. Write a function that places 50 dollar signs across the cells.
3. Write a function that removes the 50 dollar signs that were placed across the cells.

NEW COMMANDS AND KEYS

@SUM(range). Adds the contents of the cells in the range.

@AVG(range). Averages the contents of the cells in the range.

@MIN(range). Displays the minimum value in the range of cells.

@MAX(range). Displays the maximum value in the range of cells.

@COUNT(range). Counts the number of cells in the range.

@REPEAT(character string,number). Repeats a character string a specified number of times.

FILES CREATED IN THIS SECTION

PRAC6A

PRAC6B

ACT61

ACT62

ACT63

ACTIVITIES

ACTIVITY 6-1

1. Retrieve the ACT52 worksheet. Key the *functions* that will calculate the following at the designated cells. Develop the functions by pointing to cells. Write the functions you constructed in the spaces provided. Finally, repeat asterisks across the worksheet.

    [E1] The sum of A1, B1, and C1

    [E2] The sum of A1, B1, A2, and B2

    [E3] The average of A3, B3, and C3

    [E4] The average of A3, B3, A4, and B4

    [E5] The minimum value in all of Column A

    [E6] The minimum value in all of Column B

    [E7] The maximum value in cells A1, B1, A2, B2, A3, and B3

    [E8] The maximum value in all of columns A and B

    [E9] The difference between the maximum and minimum values in all of Columns A and B

    [A10] The number of cells in the range A1 through A9

    [B10] The number of cells in the range A1 through B9

2. Use the @repeat function to place asterisks (*) across the worksheet in row 11, from column A to column E.

3. Save the worksheet as ACT61 and then print it. Erase the worksheet.

(Template File: ACT62TP)

ACTIVITY 6-2

```
           A         B         C         D         E         F
 1                         STUDENT GRADES
 2
 3    STUDENT    TEST 1    TEST 2    TEST 3    TEST 4
 4
 5    Jones, L     88        86        79        89
 6    Kerr, G     100        78        90       100
 7    Slate, R     98        92        95        96
 8    Vance, P     87        75        72        80
 9    Cupp, R      77        67        71        80
10    Mays, T      68        71        73        78
11    Wilson, D    82        86        78        87
12    Weeks, A     90        74        87        88
13    Ruiz, L      94        88        86        92
14    Goins, C     95        87        85        90
```

1. On a clean worksheet, key the data shown above. Key the main title *(STUDENT GRADES)* at D1. Center the column headings.

2. Key the following labels:
   [A16] AVERAGE
   [A17] MAXIMUM
   [A18] MINIMUM

3. At B16, C16, D16, and E16, key a function that averages the grades in each column.

4. At B17, C17, D17, and E17, key a function that finds the maximum value (highest grade) in each column.

5. At B18, C18, D18, and E18, key a function that finds the minimum value (lowest grade) in each column.

6. Save the worksheet as ACT62, print it, and then erase it.

(Template File: ACT63TP)

ACTIVITY 6-3

```
         A        B             C               D          E
 1  ALLEN AUDIO
 2  3744 East Lindley           PURCHASE ORDER #3724
 3  Berkeley, CA 94708
 4
 5                  TO   DARRELL DISTRIBUTORS
 6                       Box 7712
 7                       Redmond, WA 98073
 8                                              UNIT
 9  QTY  STOCK NO   DESCRIPTION                 PRICE      AMOUNT
10
11  2    778T6421   QUADRON T64 SPEAKER          55.25
12  3    8804RS55   WOODKEN CASSETTE RECEIVER   260.99
13  2    291L7299   QUADRON CAR AMPLIFIER       155.49
14  4    4529GL88   ROC CD PLAYER               278.99
15  3    9002HL52   ROC CASSETTE DECK           315.55
16  2    723PN556   PLUM MOD 2 LOUDSPEAKER      445.99
17
```

On a clean worksheet, key the data shown on the purchase order above. Begin *PURCHASE ORDER #3724* at D2. Right align *TO* in B5. Key *DARRELL DISTRIBUTORS* in C5. Right align column headings over numeric columns (A, D, E). Widen column C to 26 spaces and column D to 10.

1. At E11 through E16, key a formula that multiplies UNIT PRICE by QTY.

2. At E17, key a function that totals the Amount column. Key the label *SUBTOTAL* at D17.

3. At E18, key a formula that calculates 5% sales tax on the order. Key 5% as .05. Key an appropriate label for the calculation at D18.

4. At E19, key a formula or function that will add the sales tax amount to the SUBTOTAL amount. Key the label *TOTAL* at D19.

5. Save the worksheet as ACT63, print it, and then erase it.

LESSON 7

Range and Global Format

OBJECTIVES

- Designate a range of cells
- Erase a range of cells
- Set range and global format of numbers
- Format a range of labels
- Set global column width

Estimated Time: 45 minutes

VOCABULARY

Comma format
Currency format
Fixed format
Override
Percent format
Range

RANGE

A **range** is a rectangular group of *adjacent* cells (cells that border or touch each other). A range may be one cell, a horizontal group of cells (in a row), a vertical group of cells (in a column), or an arrangement of both horizontal and vertical cells (rows and columns). Figure 7-1 shows the four ways cells can be grouped into a range.

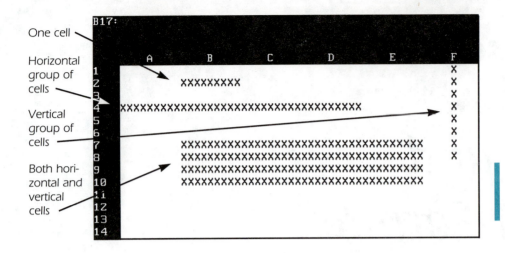

Figure 7-1
A range may be one cell or a group of adjacent cells.

You have already used ranges for printing and for establishing the argument for functions. In this lesson and the following one, you will learn more commands that involve working with a range of cells.

Use a range command when you want to perform the same operation on several adjacent cells at once. Highlight the entire range with the cursor keys (mouse), and show the end of the range with Enter (left button). *In Release 2.2, you must anchor the range with a period before highlighting the entire range.*

To cancel an incorrect or previously set anchor in any release, press (ESC), move to the proper cell, and then key a period to identify the new anchor before highlighting the range.

When resetting the anchor for a range, press Esc to cancel the previous anchor.

ERASE

You may erase the contents of a cell or a range of cells by using the **Range Erase** command. (One or two cells may be erased in Releases 2.3 and 2.4 with the (DELETE) key.) Be very careful with the Range Erase command, because it is easy to accidentally erase the wrong values.

Look carefully before completing the Range Erase command.

QUICK QUESTIONS

1. What is a range in 1-2-3?
2. What are four ways in which cells can be grouped into a range?

   a.

   b.

   c.

   d.

3. When should you use a range command?
4. What do you press to show the end of a range when using the Range Erase command?
5. What key do you press to cancel a previously set anchor?
6. What command do you use to erase a single cell or a group of cells?

Erase several ranges of cells.

1. Load 1-2-3 if necessary.
2. Retrieve the PRAC5A worksheet.

Erase the entries in rows 8 and 9 of the worksheet. Go to the beginning of the range you want to erase and then begin the Range Erase command.

3. Goto cell A8.
4. Key / **R**ange **E**rase.

The message **Enter range to erase:A8..A8** appears, as shown in Figure 7-2.

EXERCISE 7-1

Move the mouse to the control panel and click on **R**ange, **E**rase.

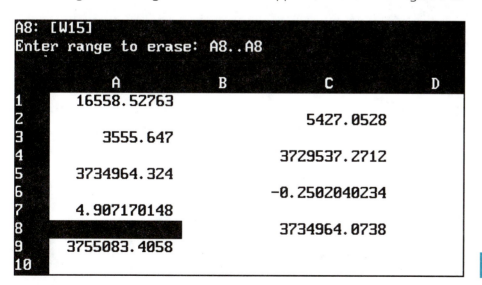

Figure 7-2
Beginning Range Erase.

5. ([A8] [.] in Release 2.2 to anchor the beginning of the range)

6. [A8] [↓] to move to cell A9 and then key [→] to move to the end of the range, C9.

Click on cell A8 and drag the mouse pointer to cell C9, the end of the range. Release the mouse button.

Note that the control panel indicates you have designated A8 through C9 as the range (see Figure 7-3).

```
C9: [W15]
Enter range to erase: A8..C9
              A              B              C              D
1      16558.52763
2                                       5427.0528
3        3555.647
4                                       3729537.2712
5      3734964.324
6                                      -0.2502040234
7       4.907170148
8                                       3734964.0738
9      3755083.4058
10
```

Figure 7-3
Ending Range Erase.

7. [C9] **ENTER** to end the range to be erased

Click the mouse button.

Rows 8 and 9 are blank; the cells have been erased.

Now, erase cells A3 through A7:

8. [A3] / **R**ange **E**rase

9. **[A3]** [.] in Release 2.2 to anchor A3 as the beginning of the range

10. [A3] [↓] to go to A7

11. [A7] **ENTER** to end the range and erase the cells

The message **ERR** appears at cell C6 because the formula at C6 refers to a cell that was just erased. The error message warns the user that a problem has developed.

12. On your own, use the **R**ange **E**rase command to erase the remaining values in column C.

13. Use the **R**ange **E**rase command to erase the value at cell A1.

The worksheet should be blank.

14. Key / **W**orksheet **E**rase **Y**es **Y**es to clear the worksheet.

FORMAT OF NUMBERS

As you have probably noticed, 1-2-3 does not always display numbers exactly as you key them. For example, if you key 345.00, the decimal point and ending zeros are omitted. As a result, columns of numbers are not aligned on the decimal point. In addition, no dollar signs or commas for large numbers are displayed. Fortunately, format commands are available to make numbers more legible and attractive.

You can display *all or most* of the numeric cells in the worksheet in a particular format by using the **Worksheet Global Format** command. Or, you can format just *some* numeric cells in a particular format by using the **Range Format** command.

Frequently used formats include: comma, currency, fixed, and percent. For each of these formats, you must determine how many decimal places you desire (from 0 to 15). If a number has more decimal places than you choose for the format, 1-2-3 will round up to the nearest number if the decimal value is .5 or more.

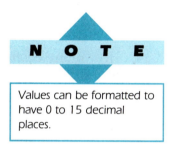

Values can be formatted to have 0 to 15 decimal places.

COMMA FORMAT

Comma format displays numbers with thousands, millions, and billions separated by commas; parentheses or a minus sign for negatives; and a leading zero for decimal values. For example, with comma format and two decimal places, the value 14556722 would be displayed as 14,556,722.00.

CURRENCY FORMAT

Currency format displays just like comma format, but currency format adds a dollar sign. For example, the number 14556722 would be displayed in currency format with two decimal places as $14,556,722.00.

FIXED FORMAT

Fixed format displays numbers with a minus sign for negatives and a leading zero for decimal values. Choose this format when you merely want to establish a particular number of decimal places and want no other formatting. The value 14556722 in fixed format with two decimal places, for example, would appear as 14556722.00.

PERCENT FORMAT

Percent format displays numbers as percentages. 1-2-3 does this by multiplying 100 times the value and adding a percent sign. For example, the value .6581, in percent format with two decimal places, would appear as 65.81%.

QUICK QUESTIONS

1. What command do you use to display all numeric cells in the worksheet in a particular format?

2. What command do you use to format just some numeric cells in a particular format?

3. What are the four most-frequently used formats?

4. How many decimal places can you have for a particular format?

5. Write this number in comma format with three decimal places: 775891330.5.

6. Write this number in currency format with no decimal places: 775891330.5.

7. Write this number in fixed format with four decimal places: 775891330.5.

8. Write this number in percent format with two decimal places: 345.772.

GLOBAL FORMAT

When most of the numbers on a worksheet should appear in a particular way, use the **Worksheet Global Format** command. This global command will change the format of all cells in the worksheet that have not been formatted with a range command. You can then format individual areas of the worksheet that should have a different appearance by using the Range Format command. A global command can be used at any position in the worksheet. Figure 7-4 shows the Global Format options.

A global command can be used at any position in the worksheet.

Set the global format for the majority of numbers in the worksheet.

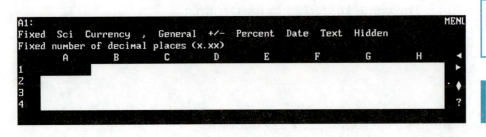

Figure 7-4
The Global Format options.

Experiment to see the effects of various global formats on a worksheet.

EXERCISE 7–2

1. Retrieve the ACT53 worksheet.

Look at the numbers in the worksheet. Column B contains money amounts. Money amounts are usually formatted in one of three ways: currency with dollar signs and no (zero) decimal places; currency with dollar signs and two decimal places; or comma with two decimal places.

First, use the global currency format command. Remember that a global format command can be used at any position in the worksheet.

2. Key / **W**orksheet **G**lobal **F**ormat **C**urrency.

3. Key **0** **ENTER** for zero decimal places.

Now the values are preceded by dollar signs. In addition, the decimal part of the values (cents) for Taxes and Net Profit After Taxes are gone; the values have been rounded off.

The worksheet would look better without so many dollar signs, and the Taxes and Net Profit After Taxes amounts are not entirely accurate. See if the global fixed format command with two decimal places gives a better appearance than the last command.

4. Key / **W**orksheet **G**lobal **F**ormat **F**ixed.

5. Key **ENTER** to accept two decimal places.

Asterisks appear across some of the numeric cells. As you will recall, this means that the number of characters in the cells exceeds the current cell width, which is nine. Next, widen the column to 12.

6. Goto column B.

7. Key / **W**orksheet **C**olumn **S**et-**W**idth **1** **2** **ENTER**.

Now the worksheet is less cluttered, but the numbers would be more readable if the thousands were set off with commas. Set the global format for comma with two decimal places instead of the present format.

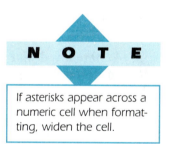
NOTE

If asterisks appear across a numeric cell when formatting, widen the cell.

8. Key / **W**orksheet **G**lobal **F**ormat **,** **ENTER**.

Keep the worksheet on your screen for the next exercise.

It is important to set the global format first, according to the format desired for *most* cells in the worksheet. You can then set a range format wherever a different format is desired.

RANGE FORMAT

Use the **Range Format** command to individually format one numeric cell or a range of numeric cells that should have a different appearance from the global format. A range format **overrides**, or sets aside, a global format; a global format never changes a range format. The Range Format options are the same as the Global Format options, as shown in Figure 7-5.

NOTE

Use the Range Format command for one numeric cell or a range of numeric cells.

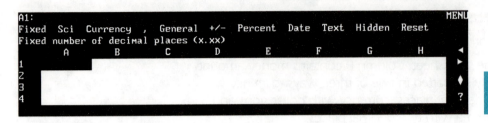

Figure 7-5
The Range Format options.

It is common practice to place dollar signs at first entry and at subtotal and total positions within a column of dollar amounts. Use the Range Format command to individually format those specific cells.

The Range Format command overrides the Global Format command.

QUICK QUESTIONS

1. Which command do you use to format most of the numbers in a worksheet?

2. Where should the pointer be when you begin a global command?

3. In what three ways are money amounts usually formatted?

    a.

    b.

    c.

4. Does a global command override a range command? Explain.

5. Where are dollar signs commonly placed within a column of dollar amounts?

    a.

    b.

    c.

▶ **EXERCISE 7–3**

Format each single-cell range below.

1. [B6] / **R**ange **F**ormat **C**urrency (ENTER) to accept 2 decimal places

2. [B6] (ENTER) to accept one cell as the range

3. [B10] / **R**ange **F**ormat **C**urrency (ENTER) to accept 2 decimal places

4. [B10] (ENTER) to accept one cell as the range

5. On your own, key the command to specify the currency format with 2 decimal places at cells B13, B18, B20, and B24.

6. Check your worksheet against Figure 7-6.

7. Save the worksheet as PRAC7A and then erase it.

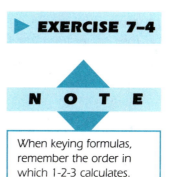

Figure 7-6
The PRAC7A worksheet.

Add a column to a worksheet and then use the range format command.

▶ EXERCISE 7-4

1. Retrieve the ACT62 worksheet.

2. [F2] % INCREASE

3. [F3] (TEST 1 TO 4)

To get the percentage of improvement from Test 1 to Test 4, subtract Test 1 from Test 4 and then divide by Test 1. The subtraction part of the formula must be in parentheses so it will be performed before the division. Point to the cells as you build the formula.

4. [F5] (**(**)

5. Point to cell E5. Key **−**.

6. Point to cell B5. Key **)**.

7. [F5] **/**

8. Point to cell B5.

9. [B5] **ENTER**

10. On your own, key similar formulas at cells F6 through F14.

It is important to show clearly that the amounts in column F are percentages. To do this, use the **R**ange **F**ormat **P**ercent command.

11. [F5] / **R**ange **F**ormat **P**ercent

12. Press **ENTER** for two decimal places.

13. **[F5] . in Release 2.2 to anchor the beginning of the range.**

14. Point to F14.

15. Key **ENTER** to end the range.

16. Check your worksheet against Figure 7-7.

N O T E

When keying formulas, remember the order in which 1-2-3 calculates.

```
A1:                                                              READY

     A        B      C       D      E      F        G      H
 1                     STUDENT GRADES
 2                                         % INCREASE
 3  STUDENT  TEST 1  TEST 2  TEST 3 TEST 4 (TEST 1 TO 4)
 4
 5  Jones, L    88     86      79     89    1.14%
 6  Kerr, G    100     78      90    100    0.00%
 7  Slate, R    98     92      95     96   -2.04%
 8  Vance, P    87     75      72     80   -8.05%
 9  Cupp, R     77     67      71     80    3.90%
10  Mays, T     68     71      73     78   14.71%
11  Wilson, D   82     86      78     87    6.10%
12  Weeks, A    90     74      87     88   -2.22%
13  Ruiz, L     94     88      86     92   -2.13%
14  Goins, C    95     87      85     90   -5.26%
15
16  AVERAGE   87.9   80.4    81.6     88
17  MAXIMUM    100     92      95    100
18  MINIMUM     68     67      71     78
19
20
```

Figure 7-7
The PRAC7B worksheet.

17. Analyze the worksheet results. Did more students increase or decrease their scores from Test 1 to Test 4?

18. Save the worksheet as PRAC7B. Keep it on your screen; you will use it in the next exercise.

FORMAT OF LABELS

When you have a range of labels that should all be right, left, or center aligned, use the **Range Label** command. If you only have an occasional cell to align, use a label prefix character. A range label command and a label prefix character can override each other; the one that was completed most recently is the one in effect.

> **NOTE**
>
> Using the Range Label command is a fast way to align a range of labels.

▶ **EXERCISE 7-5**

The column headings in the PRAC7B worksheet are centered using label prefix characters. You can override the label prefix characters with the **R**ange **L**abel command to align headings at the right.

1. [A3] / **R**ange **L**abel **R**ight

2. [A3] **.** in Release 2.2 to anchor the range

3. Point to cell F2.

4. [F2] **ENTER** to end the range

5. On your own, use the **R**ange **L**abel command to right align the labels in cells A16 through A18.

6. Leave the worksheet on your screen; you will use it in the next exercise.

GLOBAL COLUMN WIDTH

The **Worksheet Global Column-Width** command affects every column on the worksheet not previously set with the Worksheet Column Set-width command. Because the Global Column-Width command widens each column the same distance, this command is used to set the size needed for most columns in the worksheet. The Global Column-Width command can be used at any cell.

When a column needs a different width than that set with the global command, use the Worksheet Column Set-Width command.

The Worksheet Column Set-Width command overrides the Global Column-Width command.

QUICK QUESTIONS

1. What command do you use to quickly center align a range of labels?
2. Does the range label command override a label prefix character? Explain.
3. Which columns are affected by Global Column-Width?
4. Will the Global Column-Width command override the Worksheet Column Set-Width command? Explain.
5. Where should the pointer be when beginning the Global Column-Width command?

▶ **EXERCISE 7-6**

Set all columns to have a width of 11.

1. Key / **W**orksheet **G**lobal **C**olumn-**W**idth `1` `1` `ENTER`.

Now, override the Global Column-Width command with a Worksheet Column Set-Width command that will make column F large enough for the long label at F3.

2. Key / **W**orksheet **C**olumn **S**et-Width.
3. Key `→` until the column is wide enough for the label.
4. Key `ENTER` to end the column width.
5. Save the worksheet as PRAC7C and then erase the worksheet.

NEW COMMANDS AND KEYS

[ESC]. Cancels an anchor.

/ Range Erase. Erases the contents of one cell or a range of cells.

/ Worksheet Global Format. Changes the default format for the entire worksheet. It is overridden by the Range Format command.

/ Range Format. Individually formats one numeric cell or a range of numeric cells.

/ Range Label. Aligns a range of labels.

/ Worksheet Global Column-Width. Widens every worksheet column the same distance. It is overridden by the Worksheet Column Set-Width command.

FILES CREATED IN THIS LESSON

PRAC7A

PRAC7B

PRAC7C

ACT71

ACT72

ACT73

CTP7

ACTIVITIES

ACTIVITY 7-1

1. Retrieve the ACT63 worksheet.
2. Use the Range Erase command to erase cells C5, C6, and C7.
3. Key the following name and address:

   [C5] MUSIC CITY

   [C6] 3455 E. Landing Avenue

   [C7] Middleton, WI 53562
4. Edit cell D2 for Purchase Order *#3865*.
5. Use the Range Erase command to erase cells A11 through D16.
6. Key the following data in rows 11 through 16. Do not forget to press apostrophe before the labels that start with numbers in column B.

   ```
   Col. A    Col. B      Col. C                    Col. D
      3      4537GL15    ROC CD PLAYER              299.00
      6      723PN556    PLUM MOD 2 LOUDSPEAKER     445.99
      4      723LX791    PLUM MOD 5 LOUDSPEAKER     619.99
      2      902R7780    QUADRON R77 SPEAKER         99.99
      7      778T6421    QUADRON T64 SPEAKER         55.25
      4      3231KL85    LIGHTFOOT CASSETTE RECEIVER 399.50
   ```

7. Most of the numbers in the worksheet are money amounts, so use the Worksheet Global Format command for fixed with two decimal places.
8. The quantities in column A should not have decimal places. Use the Range Format command for fixed, no decimal places.
9. Globally widen all columns to 11 characters.
10. Widen column C until the label at C16 is completely displayed.
11. Narrow column A to 6.
12. Save the worksheet as ACT71. Print the worksheet and then erase it.

(Template File: ACT72TP).

ACTIVITY 7-2

```
            A              B         C          D         E
1   WEEKLY WAGE REPORT
2   PART-TIME EMPLOYEES
3   WEEK ENDED APRIL 21, 19—
4
5             EMPLOYEE   HOURS      RATE       AMOUNT
6             NUMBER     WORKED     OF PAY     PAID
7
8             313-55-8927   22      4.95
9             550-82-2591   17      5.15
10            706-21-3475   21      5.15
11            523-14-1832   30      5.1
12            312-60-9920   27      5.2
13            432-62-8819   22      5.2
14
```

1. Key the worksheet shown above. Just key the column headings; you will use the Range Label command to align them. Use label prefix characters before the Employee Numbers. (The Employee Numbers will not show in their entirety until column A is widened.)

2. Set a global column width of 7.

3. Set the width of column A wide enough for the Employee Numbers to be entirely shown.

4. Use the Range Label command to right align column headings in columns B, C, and D. Use the Range Label command to center align the column headings in column A.

5. In the Amount Paid column in cells D8 through D13, key a formula that will multiply Hours Worked times Rate of Pay. Point to cells as you build the formula.

6. At B15, key a function that will total the Hours Worked. At A15, key the label *TOTAL HOURS*.

7. At D16, key a function that will total the Amount Paid to the employees. At A16, key the label *TOTAL PAID*.

8. Most of the numbers in the worksheet are money amounts. Use a Global Format command for fixed with two decimal places.

9. Now, override the global format in column B with a Range Format command for fixed with no decimal places.

10. Use the @Repeat function to place hyphens (-) across cells B14 and D14. Use the @Repeat function to place equal signs (=) across cells A4 through D4.

11. Save the worksheet as ACT72 and then print it. You will use this worksheet in the next activity.

ACTIVITY 7-3

1. Use the ACT72 worksheet for the following week's Wage Report.
2. Use Edit to change the date to April *28*, 19—.
3. Use Range Erase to erase the Hours Worked in cells B8 through B13.
4. As you key the hours worked for this week, the worksheet will automatically show the correct Amount Paid. In addition, the totals will be updated. Key the following in cells B8 through B13:

   [B8]   27
   [B9]   33
   [B10] 22
   [B11] 30
   [B12] 30
   [B13] 20

5. Save the worksheet as ACT73. Print the worksheet and then erase it.

CRITICAL THINKING PROJECT 7

Comparison shopping at three grocery stores in your town has given you the following information. Key the data into a spreadsheet. Then use functions to find: the lowest price of each food item, the highest price of each food item, and the average price of each food item. Also use functions to find the number of grocery items and the total cost for the items at each store.

Globally format the numbers in the worksheet for fixed with two decimal places. Range format the column heading labels to right align over numeric columns. Add at least one line of decorative characters across the spreadsheet.

When your spreadsheet is complete, below the data key your evaluation of which grocery store would be the best for shopping and why; consider factors that may not be obvious.

Save the worksheet as CTP7 and then erase it from the screen. In the next lesson, you will learn to print this wide worksheet.

Item	SuperBuy	FoodRite	Kellys
2 lit Hill Dew	1.19	1.25	.99
Goody Chili	1.29	1.29	1.27
Yummy Egg Roll	1.99	2.29	2.39
Bananas lb	.45	.42	.59
Eggs large	.63	.79	.83
Smiley Milk gal	2.09	2.15	2.19
Weber Beef Stew	1.69	1.75	1.69

LESSON 8

Advanced Printing

OBJECTIVES

- Set margins for printing (2.x)
- Print a wide worksheet
- Print cell formulas
- Set a page break
- Print borders, headers, and footers
- Clear print settings

Estimated Time: 45 minutes.

In Lesson 4, you learned to print simple worksheets. In this lesson, you will learn to make your printed documents look more professional.

VOCABULARY

Border

Cell formulas

Condensed print

Footer

Header

Page break

WIDE WORKSHEETS

Often a worksheet is wider than 72 characters, the number of characters 1-2-3 will print by default on a single sheet of paper. You may make several adjustments that will allow you to print more characters on each line. Your instructor may want you to

N O T E

1-2-3 will print 72 characters on a line by default.

do one or more of the following to get a wide worksheet to fit on a single sheet of paper:

1. Use wide paper in a wide carriage printer.
2. Reset the default margins using the / Print Printer Options Margins command.
3. Use the control panel on the printer to select condensed print.
4. Use a print setup code that is different for each type of printer.
5. (Rel. 3.x only) Use print options called Advanced Layout Pitch Compressed.

In all releases, 1-2-3 uses the default margins shown in Figure 8-1.

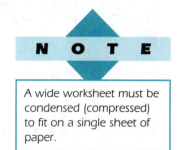

A wide worksheet must be condensed (compressed) to fit on a single sheet of paper.

Margin	Default Setting
Bottom	2 lines from the bottom of the page
Left	4 characters from the left edge of the page
Right	76 characters from the left edge of the page
Top	2 lines from the top of the page

Figure 8-1
Default margin settings.

You can change margin settings with the **Print Options Margins** command as you are preparing to print a worksheet. Figure 8-2 shows the print command menu with the subcommand menu for Options (Release 2.x).

Figure 8-2
The Print menu with the Options sub-command menu (Release 2.x).

When printing wide worksheets in Release 2.x, you must change the default margin settings. Release 3.x, however, has a special command that will condense print and automatically change the margin settings for you.

Ask your instructor how you should print wide worksheets. Write the procedure you are to follow in the space below.

Release 2.x uses the Print Options Margins Right command as a part of condensing print.

QUICK QUESTIONS

1. How many characters will 1-2-3 print on a line by default?
2. What is the default left margin setting?
3. What is the default right margin setting?
4. What is the default for top and bottom margins?
5. Write below the steps you should follow to print a wide worksheet on one sheet of paper.

▶ **EXERCISE 8-1**

Prepare a wide worksheet.

1. Load 1-2-3 if necessary.
2. Retrieve the PRAC7B worksheet.
3. Key your identification information at cell A20.
4. Set a global column width of 14.

Since PRAC7B now has six columns with a width of 14 spaces, this worksheet is too wide to fit by default on one sheet of paper. If you make no adjustments, 1-2-3 will print the first five columns on one sheet of paper and the sixth column on another sheet of paper.

5. Keep the worksheet on your screen for the following directions.

Follow Exercise 2 below if you are using 1-2-3 Release 2.x. **If you are using Release 3.x, go to Exercise 8-3 for 1-2-3 Release 3.x users, which is after the exercise below.**

(1-2-3 Release 2.x Users)

▶ **EXERCISE 8-2**

1. Check the paper in the printer for the top of the form.
2. Key **HOME** to move the pointer to cell A1 for printing.
3. Key / **P**rint **P**rinter **O**ptions **M**argins.
4. Key **R**ight to set the right margin.
5. Key **1** **3** **2** **ENTER** so the right margin will be 132 characters from the left edge of the page. (On a wide carriage printer, the right margin is often set at 240 characters.)
6. Key **Q**uit to return to the main print menu.

The margins have been reset; now you must select **condensed print**. The method of doing this varies with your situation.

7. Follow your instructor's directions now to set the print to condensed. If you do not have directions, you can set the control panel on your printer to condensed, 16 cpi, or a similar font setting.

From the main print menu, complete the print command.

8. Key **R**ange.
9. [A1] **.** to anchor A1 as the beginning of the print range

Click on cell A1 and then drag the mouse to cell F20. Release the button.

10. Key **↓** to move to A20, the bottom row of the range, and then key **TAB** to highlight the range through cell F20, the last column and row of the print range.
11. [F20] **ENTER** to designate the end of the range

Click to designate the end of the range.

12. Key **A**lign to clear for printing a new page.
13. Key **G**o to begin printing.
14. Key **P**age to eject the paper. (Printing does not have to be completed.)
15. Key **Q**uit to quit the print menu and return to Ready mode.

It is not necessary to wait for printing to be completed before returning to worksheet operations.

16. If you used the control panel on your printer to condense print, return it to normal now.
17. Save the worksheet using Replace. It will be erased when you retrieve the next worksheet.
18. Skip the exercise below (for 3.x users only) and go on to the next section, **Print Cell Formulas**.

(1-2-3 Release 3.x Users)

1. Check the paper in the printer for the top of form.
2. Key **HOME** to move the pointer to cell A1 for printing.
3. Key **/ P**rint **P**rinter **O**ptions **A**dvanced **L**ayout **P**itch **C**ompressed.
4. Key **Q**uit **Q**uit **Q**uit to return to the main Print menu.

From the main Print menu, complete the print command.

5. Key **R**ange.
6. [A1] **.** to anchor A1 as the beginning of the print range
7. Key **↓** to move to A20, the bottom row of the range, and then key **TAB** to highlight the range through cell F20, the last column and row of the print range.
8. [F20] **ENTER** to designate the end of the range
9. Key **A**lign to clear for printing a new page.
10. Key **G**o to begin printing.
11. Key **P**age to eject the paper. (Printing does not have to be completed.)

▶ **EXERCISE 8-3**

N O T E

Release 3.x uses the Print Options Advanced Layout Pitch Compressed command to condense printing. No margin setting is necessary.

12. Key **Q**uit to quit the print menu and return to Ready mode.

13. Save the worksheet using Replace. It will be erased when you retrieve the next worksheet.

PRINT CELL FORMULAS

It is often helpful to print information about the worksheet cells on the printer. A printed copy enables you to share information with others or check the accuracy of a worksheet without being at the computer. You can print cell contents with the **Print Options Other Cell-Formulas** command.

By default, 1-2-3 will print the **cell formulas** of the current print range. If the range is incorrect, press Esc to cancel it, and then reset it.

The printed list of cell formulas not only shows cell contents, but it also displays column widths and format settings. Figure 8-3 shows the cell formulas of the PRAC7A worksheet. As you can see, the cells are listed in numeric and alphabetic order. You should first find the row number and then the appropriate column letter.

> **N O T E**
>
> By default, 1-2-3 will print the cell formulas of the current print range.

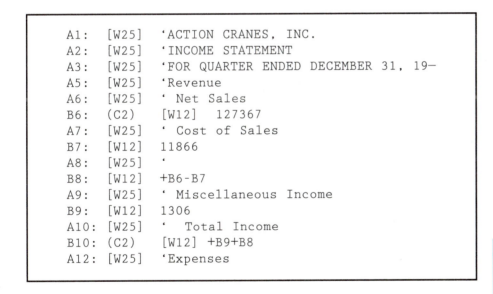

Figure 8-3
Printed cell formulas also include cell width and formatting codes.

Locate cell B6 on the sixth line in Figure 8-3. The (C2) means currency format with two decimal places. The [W12] means a column width of 12. The contents of the cell is 127367.

Locate cell B10. What is the format of the cell? _____ What is the width of the cell? _____ What are the contents of the cell? _____

LESSON 8   ADVANCED PRINTING   **99**

Print the cell formulas in the PRAC7A worksheet.

> **EXERCISE 8-4**

1. Retrieve the PRAC7A worksheet.
2. Key your identification line at cell A26.
3. Press **HOME** to move the pointer to cell A1 for printing.
4. Key **/ P**rint **P**rinter.
5. Key **R**ange.
6. If the range is correct, press **ENTER**. If it is not correct, press **ESC** to cancel it, press **.** at A1 to anchor, and then move to B26 and press **ENTER** to end the range.
7. Key **O**ptions **O**ther **C**ell-Formulas.
8. Key **Q**uit to return to the main Print menu.
9. Key **A**lign to clear for printing a new page.
10. Key **G**o to begin printing.
11. Key **P**age to eject the paper.
12. Key **Q**uit to quit the print menu and return to Ready mode. Keep the worksheet on your screen.

If the range is correct, click the button. If it is not correct, click the **right** mouse button and then click and drag the mouse until the range is correct. Release the button. Then click the button.

The Cell Formulas print option will remain with the worksheet until you change it. Return the cell formulas print option back to worksheet print using the Print Options Other As-Displayed command before you print the worksheet.

After printing cell formulas, return to worksheet printing display with the Print Options Other As-Displayed command.

QUICK QUESTIONS

1. Why is it helpful to print cell formulas on the printer?
2. What is shown in a cell formula listing?
3. What is the entire command used to print cell formulas?
4. What entire command will change cell formula printing to worksheet printing?

Return to worksheet printing.

> **EXERCISE 8-5**

1. Key **/ P**rint **P**rinter **O**ptions **O**ther **A**s-Displayed **Q**uit.

You are now at the main print menu and ready to complete the printing of the worksheet. The print range is already set from the previous printing. The print range remains with the worksheet until the range is changed.

2. Key **A**lign to clear for printing a new page.
3. Key **G**o to begin printing.

4. Key **P**age to eject the paper.

5. Key **Q**uit to quit the print menu and return to Ready mode.

6. Attach the cell formulas to your printout of the PRAC7A worksheet.

7. To save the print range with the worksheet, save the worksheet using the Replace command.

PAGE BREAK

1-2-3 has a default page length of 66 lines, which allows for the standard six lines per inch on 11-inch paper. As you saw in Figure 8-1, the top and bottom margins take 2 lines each, leaving 62 printed lines on the page. You may, however, place a specific number of lines on a page by setting a **page break** with the **Worksheet Page** command.

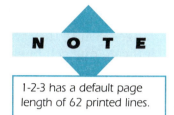

1-2-3 has a default page length of 62 printed lines.

1. Retrieve the PRAC7B worksheet.

2. Be sure your identifying information is on the worksheet, beginning in cell A21.

► EXERCISE 8-6

A page break appears as a double colon in the row where the break will occur.

You will place a page break in row 10 of the PRAC7B worksheet. To do this, you can place your pointer anywhere in row 10. After you have entered the page break, a blank row will appear with a double colon (::) in it, as shown in Figure 8-4.

```
A21: 'PRAC6B                                                    READY

7   Slate, R      98      92      95      96      -2.04%
8   Vance, P      87      75      72      80      -8.05%
9   Cupp, R       77      67      71      80       3.90%
10  ::
11  Mays, T       68      71      73      78      14.71%
12  Wilson, D     82      86      78      87       6.10%
```

Figure 8-4
A page break appears as a blank row with a double colon.

3. Move your pointer to row 10.

4. Key / **W**orksheet **P**age

   Now print the worksheet.

5. [A1] / **P**rint **P**rinter **R**ange

6. Highlight the print range, from A1 to F21.

7. [F21] **ENTER** to end the print range

8. Key **A**lign **G**o **P**age **Q**uit.

9. Remove the paper from the printer and look at the result of your page break command.

10. Keep the worksheet on your screen.

BORDERS

The second page of the worksheet printed in Exercise 8-6 is difficult to read because the columns are not labeled. This situation can be remedied by having 1-2-3 print the column headings as a border. A **border** is one or more row or column headings printed on every page of a document. Borders are set with the **Print Options Borders** command.

> **NOTE**
>
> Do not include border rows or columns in the print range.

Headings used in borders should not be included in the print range because they will print twice. Also, it is only necessary to indicate one cell in each row or column when setting the border range.

QUICK QUESTIONS

1. What does a page break look like in a worksheet?
2. What command do you use to force a new page?
3. What is a border?
4. What command do you use to set borders?

▶ **EXERCISE 8-7**

Set column borders.

1. Point to A1 (the first cell of the border range).
2. [A1] / **P**rint **P**rinter **O**ptions **B**orders **R**ows
3. [A1] [.] to anchor the beginning of the border row range
4. Point to cell A3 (the last row in the border range).
5. [A3] (ENTER) to end the range
6. Key **Q**uit to return to the main print menu.
7. Key **R**ange.
8. Press (ESC) to cancel the previous print range. The print range now must be below the border rows.
9. Point to cell A5.
10. [A5] [.] to anchor A5 as the beginning of the print range
11. Key [↓] and [→] to highlight cells A5 through F21 as the print range.
12. [F21] (ENTER) to end the print range
13. Key **A**lign **G**o **P**age **Q**uit.
14. Check page two of your document against Figure 8-5.
15. Keep the worksheet on your screen.

Click the **right** button to cancel the previous print range. Click on cell A5 and then drag the mouse to cell F21. Release the button. Then click it.

102 LESSON 8 ADVANCED PRINTING

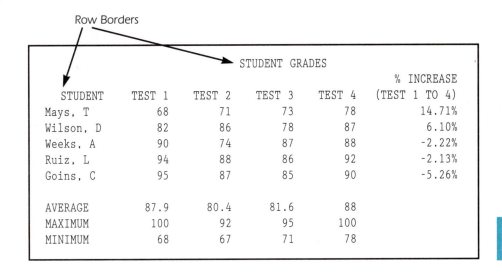

Figure 8-5
Page two printed with a row border.

HEADERS AND FOOTERS

The appearance of a printed worksheet can be enhanced by adding a date, a page number, and other important information on each page. If the information appears at the top of each page, it is called a **header**. If the information appears at the bottom of each page, it is known as a **footer**. Headers and footers are set with the **Print Options Header** and **Print Options Footer** commands.

Figure 8-6 shows the special symbols that can be used in headers and footers.

Symbol	Meaning
@	Current date
#	Page number
I (Shift-\)	Aligns items (ex: @ICOMPANY NAMEI# will center the company name and place the date at the left and the page number at the right)

Figure 8-6
Special symbols for headers and footers.

Create a header for the PRAC7B worksheet that prints **Southwest High School** and places the current date at the center. The date is indicated by the @ sign (the same symbol you use to begin functions). Then, create a footer that prints the page number, indicated by the # sign. The I sign (Shift-\) changes the placement of items to the right, left, or center.

 **EXERCISE 8–8**

1. Point to cell A1 in preparation for printing.
2. [A1] / **P**rint **P**rinter **O**ptions **H**eader
3. Key SOUTHWEST HIGH SCHOOL ⏎ @ **ENTER**.

4. Key **F**ooter.

5. Key [#] [ENTER].

6. Key **Q**uit to exit the header and footer options and return to the main print menu.

7. On your own, complete the print command.

CLEAR PRINT SETTINGS

As you may recall, print settings stay with a worksheet until it is reset if you store the worksheet on disk. When you do not want to keep special print settings, use the **Print Clear** command to remove them. Figure 8-7 shows the choices you have when using the Print Clear command.

> **NOTE**
> To place footers properly on some printers, you may have to set fewer lines per page with the Print Options Pg-Length command.

Subcommand	Purpose
All	Returns all print settings to the defaults
Range	Clears the current print range
Borders	Clears border column and row ranges
Format	Returns margins, page length, and setup string to defaults

Figure 8-7
The Print Clear command choices.

QUICK QUESTIONS

1. What term refers to information printed at the top of each page?

2. What term refers to information printed at the bottom of each page?

3. What symbol do you include in a header or footer to print a page number?

4. What symbol do you use to align header or footer items?

5. What command do you use to clear just borders from a worksheet?

6. What command do you use to clear all print settings?

Use the Print Clear All command to return all print settings to the defaults.

EXERCISE 8-9

1. Key / **P**rint **P**rinter **C**lear **A**ll **Q**uit.

2. Erase the worksheet without saving it.

NEW COMMANDS AND KEYS

/ Print Printer Options Margins. Sets left, right, top, or bottom margins; also clears all margin settings.

/ Print Printer Options Advanced Layout Pitch Compressed. In Rel. 3.x, sets the print to condensed.

/Print Printer Options Other Cell-Formulas. Prints the contents of cells, as well as width and formatting codes.

/ Print Printer Options Other As-Displayed. Prints the worksheet as it is displayed. Used to return the printing of a worksheet to normal after printing cell formulas.

/ Worksheet Page. Places a page break in the worksheet.

/ Print Printer Options Borders. Sets row or column headings to print on every page of a document.

/ Print Printer Options Header. Prints header information at the top of each page.

/ Print Printer Options Footer. Prints footer information at the bottom of each page.

@. Causes the current date to appear in a header or footer.

#. Causes the page number to appear in a header or footer.

l. Aligns items on the right, left, or center of a header or footer.

/ Print Printer Clear All Quit. Returns all print settings to the defaults.

FILES CREATED IN THIS LESSON

ACT81

ACT82A

ACT82B

ACT83

ACTIVITIES

(Template File: ACT81TP).

ACTIVITY 8-1

```
            A           B         C        D        E        F
1   ABC CORPORATION
2   PROPOSED PRODUCT PRICE INCREASES
3
4   Product #         A37889    LF88723  G55317   RS32418  GL61375
5
6   Current Price     3.47      12.99    22.42    18.65    17.98
7   % of Increase     3.2%      1.2%     8.0%     2.5%     4.4%
8   New Price
9
```

1. Key the main headings shown on the worksheet above.

2. Key the labels in column A. Widen column A so the longest data item is entirely displayed.

3. Key the labels in cells B4 through F4. Range format the labels for right alignment.

4. Set a global numeric format of currency with 2 decimal places.

5. Set cells B7 through F7 as percent format with one decimal place.

6. Enter the data shown in rows 6 and 7. Remember to key the percentages as decimal figures.

7. Compute the new prices. To do this, add 1%, the new amount of increase, to the present % of increase amount and then multiply that sum times the current price. Parentheses are needed to add before multiplying. Point to the % of Increase and Current Price cells as you develop each formula. (The formula at B8 is: (1+B7)*B6.)

8. Key an identification line at A10. The name of the worksheet is ACT81.

9. Print the worksheet. Save the worksheet as ACT81. Use the worksheet for Activity 8-2.

LESSON 8 ADVANCED PRINTING

ACTIVITY 8-2

Use the ACT81 worksheet for the following printing activities.

1. Add the following data to the ACT81 worksheet:
   ```
   [A10] Estimated Number of Sales (typeover the identi-
         fication in the cell)
   [B10] 1200
   [C10] 870
   [D10] 320
   [E10] 950
   [F10] 1300
   [A12] Estimated Sales Amount
   ```
2. Range format row 10 for fixed with 0 decimal places.
3. Widen column A if needed.
4. Set a global column width of 12.
5. Compute the estimated sales amounts by multiplying the estimated number of sales times the new price for each product.
6. Clear the print range and reset it for the length of the current worksheet. Print the wide worksheet in condensed print.
7. Print the cell formulas.
8. Save the worksheet as ACT82A. Keep it on your screen.
9. Insert a page break in row 9.
10. Set cells A1 through A4 as a row border.
11. Make a header that will display the date in the upper left corner of the page.
12. Make a footer that will display the page number at the bottom of the page.
13. (Reset the print range.) Print the worksheet.
14. Save the worksheet as ACT82B. Erase the worksheet.

ACTIVITY 8-3

Retrieve the PRAC7A worksheet. Use page breaks so the statement will print on three pages. Page one should include the revenue amounts only. Page two should include the expense amounts only. Page three should include the remaining figures at the bottom of the statement.

Set the three main heading lines as a row border for each page. Include a header that has the current date and at least one other item. Include a footer that has the page number and anything else you would like.

Print the worksheet and the cell formulas. Save the worksheet as ACT83.

*CTP7: If you completed CTP7 in the previous section, print the wide worksheet now.

LESSON 9

Changing the Worksheet with Move, Insert, and Delete

OBJECTIVES

- Move rows and columns
- Insert rows and columns
- Use Undo
- Delete rows and columns
- Split the screen into windows
- Freeze titles

Estimated Time: 50 minutes.

VOCABULARY

Dialog box Titles
Enable Window

MOVE

The **Move** command is used to place a range of cells in a new location, leaving the former location empty. Move involves *two* ranges: **Move what?** and **To where?** The *Move what* range is the range of cells you want to move. The *To where* range is where you want to place them.

The beginning of the *Move what?* range is the current cell (anchored with a period in Release 2.2), and the end is shown with Enter. For the *To where?* range, simply point to the first cell in which the range should be placed and press Enter. Because a moved range of cells must stay intact as a block, the entire block will follow the placement of the first cell.

When you are using the Move command, you must take care not to overwrite data or to move cells that would change formulas or functions in an undesirable way.

Since a moved range of cells stays intact, just point to the first cell for placement and press Enter.

N O T E

When moving cells, be careful not to overwrite data.

QUICK QUESTIONS

1. What is the purpose of the Move command?
2. What two ranges must be established for the Move command?
3. What is the *Move what?* range?
4. What is the *To where?* range?
5. What is the beginning of a *Move what?* range when using the move command?
6. What do you use to designate the end of a range when using the move command?
7. When placing moved cells, you can point to just the first cell where the range should be placed. Explain.
8. What precautions should you take when moving data?

You will move ranges, rows, and columns of data. First, move rows 18, 19, and 20 down to rows 19, 20, and 21.

1. Retrieve the PRAC6A worksheet.
2. Point to cell A18 (the first cell of the range to be moved).
3. Key / **M**ove.

The control panel message **Move what? A18...A18** appears, as shown in Figure 9-1. 1-2-3 is asking for the range of cells to be moved.

▶ **EXERCISE 9-1**

Move the mouse to the control panel and click on Move.

110 LESSON 9 CHANGING THE WORKSHEET WITH MOVE, INSERT, AND DELETE

```
A18: @AVG(A15..A6)
Move what? A18..A18
       A          B          C              D            E
1                    CUSTOMER ACCOUNT BALANCES
2
3   ACCOUNT              ACCOUNT                     PREVIOUS
4   BALANCE              NUMBER       CUSTOMER NAME  BALANCE
5
6     45.22            456-22-8874  Williams, Richard Mrs.  55.86
7    105.33            656-85-9114  Tipton, Gladys          34.4
```

Figure 9-1
Move what? appears in the control panel.

Click on cell A18, drag the mouse to cell E20, and then release the button.

4. **[A18]** `.` in Release 2.2 to anchor the beginning of the range to be moved
5. **[A18]** ↓ ↓ to move the pointer to cell A20
6. **[A20]** → → → → to move the pointer to cell E20
7. **[E20]** **ENTER** to end the **Move what?** range

Click the button to end the **Move what?** range.

The message **To where? A18** appears in the middle of the control panel, as shown in Figure 9-2. 1-2-3 wants to know where to place the cells.

```
A18: @AVG(A15..A6)
Move what? A18..E20                  To where? A18
       A          B          C              D            E
1                    CUSTOMER ACCOUNT BALANCES
2
3   ACCOUNT              ACCOUNT                     PREVIOUS
4   BALANCE              NUMBER       CUSTOMER NAME  BALANCE
5
6     45.22            456-22-8874  Williams, Richard Mrs.  55.86
7    105.33            656-85-9114  Tipton, Gladys          34.4
```

Figure 9-2
To where? appears on the control panel.

Since a moved range of cells stays intact, you need only point to the first cell where the range should be placed. Then, press **ENTER** to end the move.

8. Point to cell A19, the first cell where the range should be placed.

Move the mouse pointer to cell A19, the first cell where the range should be placed.

9. **[A19]** **ENTER** to end the **To where?** range

The range of cells has been moved. Row 18 is now empty.

Click the mouse button.

Move the labels in cells B17, B19, B20 and B21 to cells C17 through C21.

1. Move the pointer to B17, the first cell in the range to be moved.
2. Key / **M**ove.

The **Move what? B17..B17** message appears on the control panel.

3. **[B17]** `.` in Release 2.2 to anchor the beginning of the range to be moved

▶ EXERCISE 9-2

Move the mouse to the control panel and then click on Move.

LESSON 9 CHANGING THE WORKSHEET WITH MOVE, INSERT, AND DELETE

4. [B17] ⬇ ⬇ ⬇ ⬇ to highlight cells B17 through B21, the range to be moved

5. [B21] **ENTER** to end the Move what? range

The **To where? B17** message appears on the control panel.

6. Point to cell C17, the first cell of the **To where?** range.

7. [C17] **ENTER** to complete the **To where?** range.

The cells have been moved. Cells B17 through B21 are empty.

Click the mouse button on cell B17, drag the mouse to cell B21, and then release the button.

Click the mouse button.

Click on cell C17, the first cell of the **To where?** range.

Click the mouse button.

Now, move the data from column A to column B.

1. Key **HOME** to move the pointer to cell A1.

2. [A1] / **M**ove

3. **[A1] . in Release 2.2 to anchor A1 as the beginning of the move what range**

4. Move the pointer to A21, the end of the **Move what?** range.

5. [A21] **ENTER** to end the range

6. Move the pointer to cell B1, the first cell of the **To where?** range.

7. [B1] **ENTER** to complete the move

8. Save the worksheet as PRAC9A. Use it for the next activity.

▶ EXERCISE 9-3

Move the mouse to the control panel and then click on Move.

Click on cell A1, drag the mouse to cell A21, and then release the button.

Click the mouse button.

Click on cell B1, the first cell of the **To where?** range.

Click the mouse button.

INSERT ROWS AND COLUMNS

Columns or rows can be added to a worksheet with the **Worksheet Insert** command. To insert rows or columns, place the pointer on the row or column that should *move down or over* to make room for the new rows or columns. The pointer may be at any cell in the row or column that will move down or over. Then use the Worksheet Insert command.

N O T E

To begin insert, place the pointer on the row or column that should move down or over to make room for the new rows or columns.

QUICK QUESTIONS

1. What command do you use to add rows or columns to a worksheet?
2. Where should the pointer be when you begin the Worksheet Insert command?

Follow the directions to insert a single row. It would be helpful to have the company name in the heading of the PRAC9A worksheet. To make space for it, insert a row at the top of the worksheet. Place the pointer on row 1; it will move down to make room for the new row. Since you will key the company name at cell C1, begin the Worksheet Insert command there.

1. [C1] / **W**orksheet **I**nsert **R**ow
2. [C1] **ENTER** to accept one row (C1..C1) for insertion
3. [C1] PARKE'S DEPARTMENT STORE **ENTER**

Insert a new row for the date. The Worksheet Insert command can be used at any cell in row 3, but go to cell C3 to begin the command because you will key the current date there.

4. [C3] / **W**orksheet **I**nsert **R**ow
5. [C3] **ENTER** to accept one row (C3..C3) for insertion
6. [C3] Today's date (spelled out)
7. Check your work against Figure 9-3.

▶ **EXERCISE 9–4**

Move the mouse to the control panel and click on Worksheet, Insert, Row.

Click the button on cell C1 to accept one row for insertion.

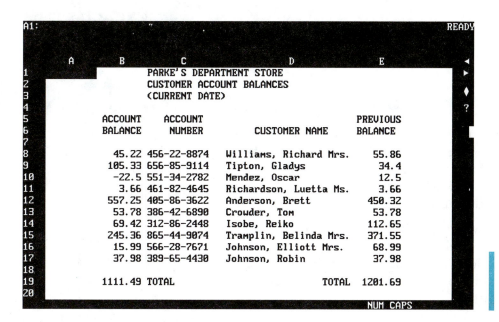

Figure 9-3
The worksheet after inserting rows for heading lines.

LESSON 9 CHANGING THE WORKSHEET WITH MOVE, INSERT, AND DELETE   113

Now, you will insert several rows. Insert three new rows at row 19. This will have the effect of moving TOTAL and the following lines down several rows. You can begin the insert command at any cell in row 19, but go to A19 for the following directions.

1. [A19] / **W**orksheet **I**nsert **R**ow

2. **[A19] [.] in Release 2.2 to anchor the beginning of the three-row range**

3. Key [↓] 2 times to highlight three rows in a downward direction.

4. [A21] [ENTER]. New rows at 19, 20, and 21 have been inserted

5. Save the worksheet as PRAC9A, using Replace. Use PRAC9A for the next activities.

Move the mouse pointer to the control panel and click on Worksheet, Insert, Row.

Click on cell A19, drag the mouse to cell A21, and release the button.

Click the mouse button.

UNDO

Your most recent operation can be reversed if you **enable** (turn on) the **Undo** feature. Undo must be enabled for each work session unless your instructor has you set it as a permanent feature. Because Undo requires a lot of memory to run, you may be unable to use the feature on your computer. Ask your instructor if you should follow the directions below for enabling and using Undo. If not, skip the following exercise.

To cancel your most recent action or command with Undo, press [ALT] [F4]. In Rel. 3.x, you must verify with *Y* for *Yes*.

Enable your Undo feature now if so instructed.

Key / **W**orksheet **G**lobal **D**efault **O**ther **U**ndo Enable Quit

N O T E

After Undo is enabled, press Alt-F4 to undo your last operation.

▶ **EXERCISE 9–5**

DELETE ROWS AND COLUMNS

Entire rows and columns may be deleted using the **Worksheet Delete** command. When you use the command, the pointer may be at any cell in the first row or column to be deleted. Formulas and functions indirectly affected by the deletions will have their cell addresses updated automatically.

You must be careful when deleting so you do not erase data by mistake. Even with Undo, deleted rows and columns cannot be restored unless the deletion is the last action. It is wise to save a worksheet before deleting, so you can return to the previous version if you delete by mistake.

N O T E

Cell addresses update automatically after deletions unless cells referred to directly are deleted.

N O T E

Always save your worksheet before making deletions.

QUICK QUESTIONS

1. a. What feature allows you to reverse the last operation?
   b. How is it enabled?
   c. What do you press to cancel your most recent action or command?

2. What command do you use to delete rows or columns in a worksheet?

3. If you are going to delete row 5, where should your pointer be when you begin the delete command?

4. When deleting columns and rows, what happens to formulas and functions that are indirectly affected?

5. What should you do before deleting rows or columns to protect against accidental deletion?

It is wise to save a worksheet before deleting, but since you recently saved the PRAC9A worksheet, it is not necessary to save it now.

EXERCISE 9-6

Follow the directions to delete a single column. Since column A is empty, delete it. You may begin the column deletion at any cell in column A, but go to cell A1.

1. [A1] / **W**orksheet **D**elete

2. Look at the choices on the control panel: **Column** and **Row**. Be very careful that you choose **Column**, not **Row** for this deletion.

3. [A1] **C**olumn

4. Key **ENTER** to accept a one-column range (A1..A1).

Column A has been deleted. **If you are using Undo, key the following to restore the deletion. After that, delete the column once more. Then use Undo whenever it is needed.**

5. [A1] **ALT** **F4** (<y> to verify in Rel. 3.x) to cancel the deletion with Undo

6. **If you cancelled the deletion with Undo, repeat the steps above to delete column A again.**

7. Check your work against Figure 9-4.

Move the mouse to the control panel, and then click on Worksheet, Delete.

Click on Column.

Click the mouse button on cell A1 to accept a one-column range (A1..A1).

```
A1:                                                    READY

       A         B              C              D        E
1            PARKE'S DEPARTMENT STORE
2            CUSTOMER ACCOUNT BALANCES
3            (CURRENT DATE)
4
5      ACCOUNT   ACCOUNT                       PREVIOUS
6      BALANCE   NUMBER      CUSTOMER NAME     BALANCE
7
8       45.22 456-22-8874  Williams, Richard Mrs.  55.86
9      105.33 656-85-9114  Tipton, Gladys          34.4
10     -22.5  551-34-2782  Mendez, Oscar           12.5
11       3.66 461-82-4645  Richardson, Luetta Ms.   3.66
12     557.25 405-86-3622  Anderson, Brett        450.32
13      53.78 386-42-6890  Crowder, Tom            53.78
14      69.42 312-86-2448  Isobe, Reiko           112.65
15     245.36 865-44-9074  Tramplin, Belinda Mrs. 371.55
16      15.99 566-28-7671  Johnson, Elliott Mrs.   68.99
17      37.98 389-65-4430  Johnson, Robin          37.98
```

Figure 9-4
The worksheet after deleting column A.

Now, follow the directions to delete a single row. Delete empty row 23. Be careful to choose **R**ow this time.

1. Point to cell A23.
2. [A23] / **W**orksheet **D**elete **R**ow
3. [A23] (ENTER) to accept one row for deletion

Follow the directions to delete several rows. Delete the three rows you previously inserted, rows 19 through 21. Begin the command at cell A19.

4. Goto A19.
5. [A19] / **W**orksheet **D**elete **R**ow
6. [A19] (.) in Release 2.2 to anchor the beginning of the range
7. Point to A21 and press (ENTER) to end the range.
8. Key an identification line at A24. Save the worksheet as PRAC9B.
9. Print the worksheet.

▶ **EXERCISE 9–7**

Move the mouse to the control panel and then click on Worksheet, Delete, Row.

Click the mouse button on cell A23 to accept one row for deletion.

Move the mouse to the control panel and then click on Worksheet, Delete, Row.

Click on cell A19, drag the mouse to cell A21, and then release the button. Click the button to end the range.

VIEWING WITH WINDOW AND TITLES

When a worksheet is wide, the **Worksheet Window** feature can be useful. Because **Window** splits the worksheet display horizontally or vertically at the pointer position, two parts of the worksheet can be viewed simultaneously (see Figure 9-5).

Window allows you to view two parts of the worksheet at the same time.

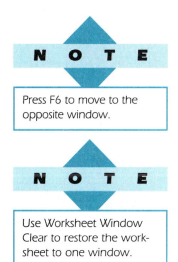

Figure 9-5
Setting a vertical window.

To set a horizontal window, place the pointer on the row you want to use as the top edge of the bottom window. To set a vertical window, place the pointer on the column you want to use as the left edge of the right window. Then, use F6 to move the pointer from one window to the other.

A split window can be restored to one window by using the **Worksheet Window Clear** command.

In Releases 2.3 and 2.4, the F6 key can also be used to remove a dialog box from view. A **dialog box** *is a screen that shows the current settings associated with a task such as printing.*

> **NOTE**
> Press F6 to move to the opposite window.

> **NOTE**
> Use Worksheet Window Clear to restore the worksheet to one window.

QUICK QUESTIONS

1. What command do you use to split the worksheet into two windows?

2. When would the Window command be useful?

3. What key do you press to move to the other window?

4. What command do you use to restore the worksheet to one window?

EXERCISE 9-8

1. Retrieve the PRAC7B worksheet.

Widen the worksheet by widening the columns to 15 characters.

2. Key **/ W**orksheet **G**lobal **C**olumn-Width **1 5**.

Because the PRAC7B worksheet is wider than your computer screen, the screen scrolls as you move your pointer from one side of the worksheet to the other.

3. Move the pointer to any cell in column C.

4. Key **/ W**orksheet **W**indow **V**ertical.

The pointer is in the left window, as shown in Figure 9-5 on page 117.

5. Key **→** to move right.

Note that your pointer is still in the left window. Now, move the pointer to the right window.

6. Key **F6**.

The pointer is now in the right window.

7. Key **←** and **→** to move from column to column in the right window.

8. Key **↓** and **↑** to move from row to row.

Return to one window.

9. Key **/ W**orksheet **W**indow **C**lear.

Now, split the worksheet horizontally.

10. Point to any row.

11. Key **/ W**orksheet **W**indow **H**orizontal.

12. Move the pointer around in each window. Clear the windows when you are done.

TITLES

Another useful feature for wide worksheets is the **Worksheet Titles** command. *Horizontal* titles freezes the display of one or more rows, and *vertical* titles freezes one or more columns. This enables you to see the frozen rows and/or columns at all times as you scroll through the rest of the worksheet. You can also use titles while you are using windows.

To set horizontal titles, place the pointer one row below the rows you want to freeze. To set vertical titles, place the pointer one column to the right of the columns you want to freeze.

The **Worksheet Titles Clear** command unfreezes the display.

Titles is often used to freeze labels necessary to identify data.

> **QUICK QUESTIONS**
>
> 1. What is the purpose of the Worksheet Titles command?
> 2. Where should your pointer be located when you set vertical titles?
> 3. What command will clear frozen titles?

EXERCISE 9-9

Use the Worksheet Titles command.

1. Move the pointer to column B.
2. Key / **W**orksheet **T**itles **V**ertical.
3. Key  to move to the right edge of the worksheet.

Note that no matter how far you move the pointer right, column A still remains in view on the left, as shown in Figure 9-6.

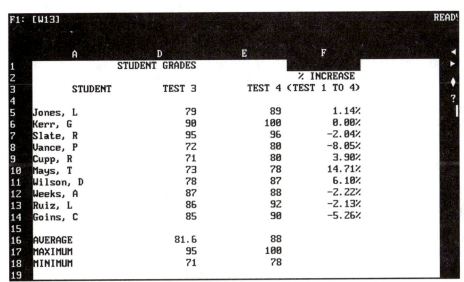

Figure 9-6
The worksheet with vertical titles that freeze column A.

Clear the vertical titles and then set horizontal titles.

4. Key / **W**orksheet **T**itles **C**lear.
5. Move the pointer to row 5.
6. Key / **W**orksheet **T**itles **H**orizontal.
7. Key ↓ to move down beyond the lower edge of the worksheet.

Regardless of the distance you move downward, the horizontal titles remain visible. This is particularly useful when you have a long worksheet.

8. Clear the horizontal titles. Do not save the worksheet.

Use Titles Clear to unfreeze rows and/or columns.

Use the Titles and Windows commands whenever you feel they will be helpful as you complete your worksheets.

LESSON 9 CHANGING THE WORKSHEET WITH MOVE, INSERT, AND DELETE

NEW COMMANDS AND KEYS

/ Move. Places a range of cells in a new location, leaving the former location empty.

/ Worksheet Insert. Adds columns or rows to a worksheet.

Undo. Feature that can reverse the most recent worksheet operation.

Alt-F4. Activates Undo if Undo has been enabled.

/ Worksheet Delete. Deletes rows or columns from a worksheet.

/ Worksheet Window Vertical. Splits the worksheet display vertically at the pointer position.

F6. Moves the pointer from one window to the other when the worksheet display is split into windows.

/ Worksheet Window Clear. Restores the worksheet display to one window.

/ Worksheet Window Horizontal. Splits the worksheet display horizontally at the pointer position.

/ Worksheet Titles Vertical. Freezes the display of one or more columns so they remain visible at all times as the worksheet scrolls.

/Worksheet Titles Clear. Unfreezes frozen titles.

/Worksheet Titles Horizontal. Freezes the display of one or more rows so they remain visible at all times as the worksheet scrolls.

FILES CREATED IN THIS SECTION

PRAC9A

PRAC9B

ACT91

ACT92

ACT93

CTP9

ACTIVITIES

ACTIVITY 9-1

1. Retrieve the ACT71 worksheet.
2. The owner of Allen Audio would like to have the stock number column first and the quantity column second. To make the switch, you must add a column to store data temporarily.
3. Insert a column at B.
4. Move cells A9 through A16 to B9 through B16.
5. Move the stock number data to column A. Widen column A if necessary.
6. In step 7, you will delete extra column C, which will erase the label TO at C5. Move the label to cell B5 now.
7. Delete empty column C.
8. Move the purchase order # labels to cells D1 and E1.
9. Insert a row at present row 17 to leave a blank row above the subtotal.
10. Erase the previous identification and key the new identification at cell A21.
11. Save the worksheet as ACT91.
12. Print the worksheet.

(Template File: ACT92TP)

ACTIVITY 9-2

```
           A              B          C          D          E          F
 1.  RELIABLE INSURANCE COMPANY
 2.  7781 PARKVIEW PLACE
 3.  ORADEL, NJ 07649
 4.
 5.  Type of loss:  Collision         Insured:  Bo Leeds
 6.  Date of loss:  08/24/—           Description:  1992 Pontiac LeMans 4dr nb sed
 7.  Assessed by:   Lou Daniels       License:  99H3992
 8.                            DOLLAR            LABOR      PART       LABOR
 9.  DESCRIPTION              AMOUNT  OPERATION  TYPE       NUMBER     UNIT
10.
11.  R QUARTER OUTER PANEL            REPAIR     BODY                  2.5
12.  R QUARTER PANEL OUTSIDE          REFINISH   REFIN                 2.1
13.  COMB LAMP FINISH PANEL           REPAIR     BODY                  0.5
14.  FINISH PANEL                     REFINISH   REFIN                 1.9
15.  R COMB LAMP HOUSING       72.00  REMOV/REPL BODY       16500184   0.4
16.  R COMB LAMP LENS          75.75  REMOV/REPL BODY       16501848   INCL
17.  REAR BUMPER COVER         65.75  REMOV/REPL BODY       **5103     2.0
18.  REAR COVER                       REFINISH   REFIN                 2.5
```

As you complete this activity, use the Titles and Windows features to help you more easily view portions of the wide worksheet.

1. To begin the worksheet shown above, widen column A to 23, column C to 11, column D to 7, and column E to 11. Then key the data. Format the numeric columns to achieve the format shown. Use the current year in the date.

2. Use the move command to move the heading lines (A1-A3) to the right so they are visually centered over the worksheet.

3. Insert a row above the column headings.

4. Move the range of cells that includes the Insured, Description, and License data to begin in column C instead of column D.

5. Save the file before you begin moving more data. Save the worksheet as ACT92.

6. Move the columns of data into the following arrangement. Insert blank columns where needed for moving. If things get scrambled, retrieve the worksheet you saved and begin again.

   ```
   LABOR                              PART     DOLLAR   LABOR
   TYPE    OPERATION   DESCRIPTION    NUMBER   AMOUNT   UNIT
   ```

7. When moving is complete, use commands to make columns as narrow as possible, display the main heading centered, and display the data in rows 5 to 7 in columns A and D.

8. When the worksheet looks attractive, save it as ACT92 using Replace.

9. Print the worksheet.

ACTIVITY 9-3

1. Retrieve the ACT92 worksheet.
2. Add the following at the cells shown. Use the space bar five times to indent the labels at A23, D22, and D23. Right align the labels at C21, F21, G21, and H21. Format all dollar ranges for fixed, two decimal places. Do not format the Units ranges; they should have one decimal place. Set column B to a width of 14.

Cell	Content
A21	Part Repl Summary
A22	Taxable Parts
A23	Sales Tax @ 5%
A24	Total Repl Parts Amts
C21	Amount (right aligned)
D21	Labor (right aligned)
D22	Body
D23	Refinish
D25	Labor Summary
E24	Labor Subtotals
F21	Units (Right align)
G21	Rate (Right align)
G22	28.00 (Format fixed, 2 decimal places)
G23	28.00 (Format fixed, 2 decimal places)
H21	Totals (Right align)

3. Key formulas and functions at the following cells. Remember, when adding adjacent cells, use the @SUM function. When adding cells that are scattered throughout the sheet, construct an addition formula by pointing to cells.

    - **C22** All parts are taxable, so add together the figures in the Dollar Amount column.
    - **C23** Figure the tax amount by multiplying the tax rate times the Taxable Parts Amount. Remember to change a percent to a decimal.
    - **C24** Total the Taxable Parts Amount and the Sales Tax Amount.
    - **F22** Body Units includes all Labor Units with BODY in the Labor Type column. These figures are scattered in column F. Point to each one as you build the formula.
    - **F23** Refinish Units includes all Labor Units with REFIN in the Labor Type column. These figures are scattered in column F. Point to each one as you build the formula.
    - **F25** Add the Units figures in cells F22 and F23.
    - **H22** Multiply the Body Units times the Body Rate.
    - **H23** Multiply the Refinish Units times the Refinish Rate.
    - **H24** Add the Body and Refinish Totals (H22 and H23).
    - **H25** Multiply the total Units at cell F25 by the Rate at either cell G22 or cell G23.

4. Save the worksheet as ACT93.
5. Print the wide worksheet.
6. Print the cell formulas. Attach them to the worksheet.

> Retrieve the ACT72 worksheet. Move, insert, and delete rows and columns where needed for the ACT72 worksheet to look like the worksheet that follows. Notice that a record for a new employee has been added to the worksheet. When complete, save the worksheet on your disk as CTP9. Print the worksheet.

CRITICAL THINKING PROJECT 9

```
RYAN-MELLON, INC.
WEEKLY WAGE REPORT
PART-TIME EMPLOYEES
WEEK ENDED APRIL 21, 19—
```

DEPT	EMPLOYEE NUMBER	HOURS WORKED	OVERTIME HOURS	RATE OF PAY	AMOUNT PAID
60	313-55-8927	22	0	4.95	108.90
45	550-82-2591	17	0	5.15	87.55
45	706-21-3475	21	0	5.15	108.15
72	496-72-0998	15	0	5.55	83.25
17	523-14-1832	30	0	5.10	153.00
40	312-60-9920	27	0	5.20	140.40
40	432-62-8819	22	0	5.20	114.40
TOTAL HOURS		154			
TOTAL OVERTIME			0		
TOTAL PAID					795.65

LESSON 10

Changing the Worksheet with Copy and Repeat Characters

OBJECTIVES

- Copy labels
- Copy numbers relative and absolute
- Repeat characters

Estimated Time: 50 minutes.

VOCABULARY

Absolute cell address
Absolute copy
Constant
Relative copy
Repeat characters

COPY

The **Copy** command copies data from one place to another, resulting in data in both places. It is used for labels, numbers, formulas, or functions. Copy involves *two* ranges: *Copy what?* and *To where?*. The **Copy what** range is the range of cells you want to copy. The **To where** range is where you want to place the copied cells.

You must be careful when copying so that other data is not accidentally overwritten. Sometimes copying places zeros or the message ERR in cells because the copy has changed formulas or functions to refer to non-numeric cells, among other problems. If this occurs, just go to the cell with the zeroes or ERR message and press **DELETE** or use the Range Erase command.

If copying places zeros or ERR in blank cells, just erase them.

COPY LABELS

In the following exercise, you will copy a range of labels. First, set the *Copy what?* and then the *To where?* range.

1. Retrieve the PRAC6A worksheet.

First, erase the labels at D17 through D20.

2. Goto cell D17.

3. [D17] **R**ange **E**rase

4. **[D17]** **.** in Release 2.2 to anchor D17 as the beginning of the range to be erased.

5. [D20] **ENTER** to end the range to be erased

Copy the labels from B17 through B20 to the empty cells.

6. Goto B17 to begin the copy procedure.

7. [B17] / **C**opy

The message **Copy what? B17..B17** appears on the control panel (as shown in Figure 10-1).

▶ **EXERCISE 10-1**

Click on cell D17.

Roll the mouse to the control panel and then click on Range, Erase.

Click on cell D17, drag the mouse to cell D20, and then release the mouse button.

Click the mouse button to end the range to be erased.

Click on cell B17.

Roll the mouse to the control panel and then click on Copy.

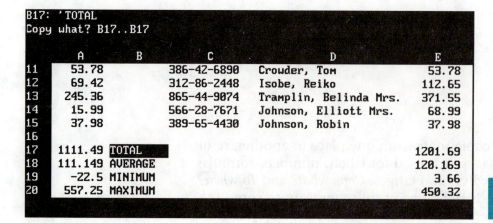

Figure 10-1
The **Copy what?** message.

Next, set the beginning and end of the range of cells to be copied.

8. [B17] (.) in Release 2.2 to anchor the beginning of the what range

9. Move the pointer to cell B20.

10. [B20] **ENTER** to end the **Copy what?** range

The **To where?** message appears at the center of the control panel, as shown in Figure 10-2.

Click on cell B17, drag the mouse to cell B21, and then release the mouse button.

Click the mouse button to end the **Copy what?** range.

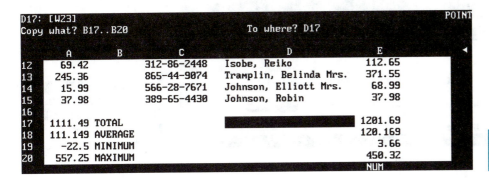

Figure 10-2
The **To where?** message.

Because a copied range of cells stays intact, you need only point to the first cell where the range should be placed. Then, press **ENTER** to complete the move.

11. Point to cell D17 (the first cell where the range should be placed).

12. [D17] **ENTER** to end the **To where?** range

13. To improve the appearance of the moved labels, use the **R**ange **L**abel **R**ight command to right align them.

14. Save the worksheet as PRAC10A. Use it for the next exercise.

Click on cell D17 (the first cell where the range should be placed).

Click the mouse button to end the **To where?** range.

COPY FORMULAS

The procedure for copying formulas is the same as copying labels. You must set *Copy what?* and *To where?* ranges.

In column F, find the difference between the current account balance (column A) and the previous account balance (column E) for each customer. Key the formula once, and then copy it for all customers.

What formula would you use to find the difference between the values in cells A6 and E6?

Enter the following data and formula into the PRAC10A worksheet.

1. [F3] BALANCE

2. [F4] CHANGE

3. [F6] (+)

4. Point to cell A6 (or click on cell A6 with the mouse button).

5. [A6] (−)

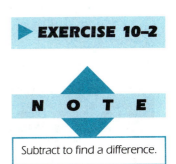

Subtract to find a difference.

LESSON 10 CHANGING THE WORKSHEET WITH COPY AND REPEAT CHARACTERS **127**

6. Point to E6 (or click on cell E6 with the mouse button).

7. [E6] **ENTER** (or click the mouse button)

The formula appears on the contents line, and the result of the formula appears in the cell. Since the current balance is smaller than the previous balance, there is a negative difference. This is shown as -10.64 (see Figure 10-3).

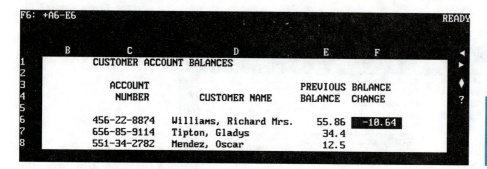

Figure 10-3
The formula appears on the contents line. The result appears in the worksheet cell.

Copy the formula to cells F7 through F15.

8. [F6] / **C**opy

The answer to **Copy what?** is the formula at F6, which is shown on the control panel as F6..F6, a one-cell range.

Click on cell F6. Roll the mouse to the control panel and then click on Copy.

9. [F6] **ENTER** to accept F6..F6 as the **Copy what?** range

The message **To where?** appears. Since the pointer is on cell F6, F6 appears with the message, but we want to begin placing the formula in empty cell F7.

Click the mouse button to accept F6..F6 as the **Copy what?** range.

10. Point to cell F7.

11. [F7] **.** in all releases to anchor the beginning of the **To where?** range

12. Point to cell F15.

Click on cell F7, drag the mouse to cell F15, and then release the mouse button.

13. [F15] **ENTER** to end the **To where?** range, completing the copy

Look at the contents line to see the contents of cells F6 through F15. The formula in row 6 has cell addresses A6 and E6. When the formula was copied down one row to row 7, the cell addresses changed one row, to A7 and E7. In Figure 10-4, you can see cell F7 (the current cell) and its contents (+A7-E7).

Click the mouse button to end the **To where?** range, completing the copy.

The formula appears on the contents line, and the result of the formula appears in the cell.

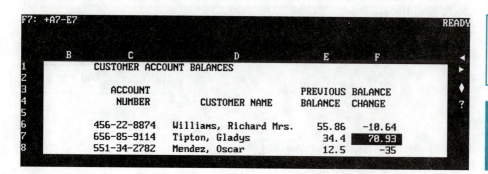

Figure 10-4
When the formula was copied down one row, the cell addresses changed one row.

The formula in row 8 has cell addresses of A8 and E8, reflecting the copy one row below A7 and E7, and so on, for each cell copied to.

14. Save the worksheet as PRAC10B. Use the worksheet for the next exercise.

RELATIVE COPY

When 1-2-3 copies a function or a formula containing cell addresses, by default it copies **relative** to the new row or column in which it is placed. That is why the cell addresses matched the row they were in after the copy in the exercise above. (In row 6 the row numbers were 6, as in **A6-E6**; in row 7 the row numbers were 7, as in **A7-E7**).

Because the copy command copies relative, it is important to use cell addresses rather than actual numbers in a cell. Look frequently at the cell contents on the control panel as you copy to see the column letters and row numbers change as you copy, to verify that the cell addresses change correctly.

NOTE

After a formula is copied relative, the cell addresses reflect their new location.

QUICK QUESTIONS

1. What is the purpose of the Copy command?
2. What two ranges must you establish when using the Copy command?
3. What is the **Copy what?** range?
4. What is the **To where?** range?
5. What should you do if copying places zeros in blank cells?
6. After you copy a formula, where does the formula appear?
7. After you copy a formula, where does the result of the formula appear?
8. What does -10.64 mean as the result of a subtraction formula?
9. What is meant by relative copy?
10. Assume that at cell C3 you have the following formula: +C3-B3. You copy the formula relative into cells C4 through C10. What formula will appear at cell C7?

COPY FUNCTIONS

Functions are copied like labels and formulas, using *Copy what?* and *To where?* ranges.

Copy the functions at E17 through E20 into cells F17 through F20.

1. Point to cell E17.
2. [E17] / **C**opy

The answer to **Copy what?** is the range of cells from E17 through E20.

3. **[E17]** `.` in Release 2.2 to anchor E17 as the beginning of the **Copy what?** range
4. Point to cell E20.
5. **[E20]** (**ENTER**) for the end of the **Copy what?** range

To where? is the range of cells from F17 through F20. You need only point to the first cell where the range will be placed.

6. Point to cell F17.
7. **[F17]** (**ENTER**) to end the **To where?** range

Look at the contents line for cell F17. The column letter in the function's cell addresses is F, the column the function is in. When the @SUM function was copied from column E to column F, the column letter in the cell addresses changed to F, **relative** to the column where the function was placed. Move to the other functions in cells F18 through F20. You will see that the functions are copied relative to their new locations.

8. Check your worksheet against Figure 10-5.

EXERCISE 10-3

Click on cell E17.

Move the mouse to the control panel and then click on Copy.

Click on cell E17, drag the mouse to cell E20, and then release the mouse button.

Click the mouse button for the end of the **Copy what?** range.

Click on cell F17.

Click the mouse button to end the **To where?** range.

```
F1:                                                          READY

       B          C              D              E        F
1                 CUSTOMER ACCOUNT BALANCES
2
3                 ACCOUNT                    PREVIOUS BALANCE
4                 NUMBER       CUSTOMER NAME  BALANCE  CHANGE
5
6                 456-22-8874  Williams, Richard Mrs.   55.86   -10.64
7                 656-85-9114  Tipton, Gladys           34.4     70.93
8                 551-34-2782  Mendez, Oscar            12.5    -35
9                 461-82-4645  Richardson, Luetta Ms.    3.66     0
10                405-86-3622  Anderson, Brett         450.32   106.93
11                386-42-6890  Crouder, Tom             53.78     0
12                312-86-2448  Isobe, Reiko            112.65   -43.23
13                865-44-9074  Tramplin, Belinda Mrs.  371.55  -126.19
14                566-28-7671  Johnson, Elliott Mrs.    68.99   -53
15                389-65-4430  Johnson, Robin           37.98     0
16
17     TOTAL                            TOTAL         1201.69   -90.2
18     AVERAGE                          AVERAGE        120.169   -9.02
19     MINIMUM                          MINIMUM          3.66  -126.19
20     MAXIMUM                          MAXIMUM        450.32   106.93
                                                         NUM CAPS
```

Figure 10-5
Worksheet check after copying functions.

9. Save the worksheet as PRAC10B. Use Replace. Keep the worksheet on your screen for the next exercise.

COPY ABSOLUTE

As you have seen, by default 1-2-3 copies functions and formulas with cell addresses relative to their new locations. Sometimes, however, you may want one or more of the cell addresses in a formula or function to remain **constant** when it is copied. You may achieve an **absolute copy** by using an **absolute** (unchanging) **cell address**.

If a formula contains an absolute cell address, that address will remain intact when the formula is copied. An absolute cell address has a dollar sign *before* both the column letter and the row number. The F4 function key will place dollar signs in the address so you do not have to do it manually. (You can also make just the row number absolute, as A$3, or just the column letter absolute, as $A3.)

QUICK QUESTIONS

1. By default, does 1-2-3 copy relative or absolute?
2. When should you use absolute copy?
3. How is an absolute copy achieved?
4. What is special about the appearance of an absolute cell address?
5. What key is the absolute key?

Use a formula that contains an absolute cell address to find the percentage each customer's previous balance is of the total previous balance. You want the customer balance to change with each customer, but the total balance should remain constant.

What type of calculation is used to find a percentage? (addition, subtraction, multiplication, or division)

Key the following data and formula into the PRAC10B worksheet. Then copy the formula.

1. [G3] PERCENT
2. [G4] OF TOTAL
3. Point to G6 and then press [+].
4. Point to E6 and then press [/].

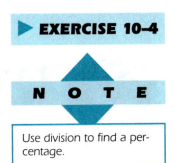

▶ **EXERCISE 10-4**

N O T E

Use division to find a percentage.

Click on G6 and then press <+>.

Click on E6 and then press </>.

LESSON 10   CHANGING THE WORKSHEET WITH COPY AND REPEAT CHARACTERS   **131**

5. Point to E17 and then press **F4** to place dollar signs with the cell address.

Refer to the contents line of Figure 10-6.

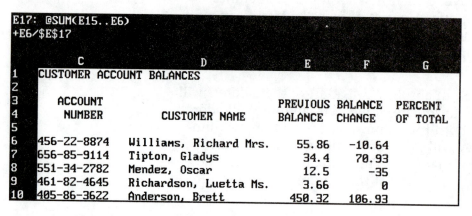

Click on E17 and then press **F4** to place dollar signs with the cell address.

Figure 10-6
Press F4 to place dollar signs for an absolute cell address.

6. Press **ENTER** to end the calculation.

Note that the percentage is shown as a decimal figure. Next, copy the formula down column G.

7. [G6] / **C**opy

8. [G6] **ENTER** to accept one cell, G6..G6, as the **Copy what?** range.

Next, set the **To where?** range.

9. Point to G7 and then press **.** to anchor G7 as the beginning of the **To where?** range.

10. Point to G15 and then press **ENTER** to show the end of the **To where?** range.

11. Key **↓** to view the contents of the cells.

The first cell address in the formula should have changed relative to its position (E_x), but the second cell address should not have changed (E17). Check your work against Figure 10-7.

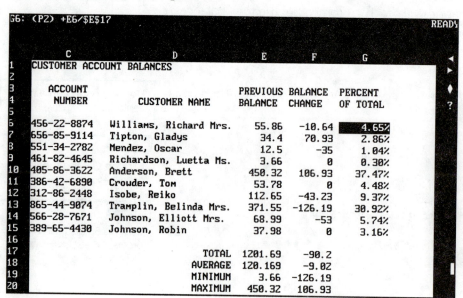

Click the mouse button to end the calculation.

Click on cell G6, move the mouse to the control panel, and then click on Copy.

Click the mouse to accept one cell, G6..G6, as the **Copy what?** range.

Click on cell G7, drag the mouse to cell G15, and then release the button.

Click the button to show the end of the **To where?** range.

Figure 10-7
Worksheet check after absolute copy.

12. On your own, format the Percent of Total column for percent format with two decimal places.

13. Save the file as PRAC10B. Use **R**eplace. Keep the worksheet on your screen for the next exercise.

REPEAT CHARACTERS

One of the simplest ways to enhance the appearance of a worksheet is by using **Repeat Characters.** Repeat Characters is a feature that fills a cell with one or more characters.

Although it can be used to repeat any characters, the Repeat Characters feature is often used to underline or visually separate parts of the worksheet. The Repeat Characters feature differs from the @REPEAT function in that Repeat Characters always fills an entire cell.

To repeat characters, press \ (inverted slash), key the character(s), and then press [ENTER]. This will repeat the character(s) across one cell. After a cell is filled with repeat characters, you can copy it to other locations.

> **NOTE**
>
> After formatting for percent, check that the percent values are reasonable and not too large.

> **NOTE**
>
> Repeat characters fills a cell with one or more characters.

QUICK QUESTIONS

1. What is the purpose of the Repeat Characters feature?
2. How does the Repeat Characters feature differ from the @REPEAT function?
3. What key do you press to begin the Repeat Characters feature?
4. After you fill a cell with repeat characters, what can you do to place the same repeat characters in other locations?

Except for directory paths, the inverted slash (\) in 1-2-3 is used only for Repeat Characters.

Place a ruling in cells A16 and E16 through G16 above the total amounts.

1. [A16] [ENTER] to fill the cell with hyphens

Next, copy the repeat characters label to cell E16. First, set the **Copy what?** range.

2. [A16] / **C**opy [ENTER] to complete the **Copy what?** range of one cell

Set the **To where?** range.

3. Point to cell E16.
4. [E16] [.] to anchor the **To where?** range

▶ **EXERCISE 10–5**

Click on cell A6, roll the mouse to the control panel, and click on Copy. Then click the mouse button to complete the **Copy what?** range of one cell.

5. Point to G16.
6. [G16] **ENTER** to complete the **To where?** range

Click on cell E6, drag the mouse to cell G16, and then release the button.

Now, place decorative borders above and below the column headings.

7. [A2] **** **=** **ENTER** to fill the cell with equal signs

Click the mouse button to complete the **To where?** range.

Set the **Copy what?** range.

8. [A2] / **C**opy **ENTER** to complete the **Copy what?** range

Set the **To where?** range.

9. Point to cell B2, the first cell where the range should be placed.
10. [B2] **.** to anchor the beginning of the **To where?** range
11. Point to cell G2.
12. [G2] **ENTER** to end the **To where?** range
13. Check your worksheet against Figure 10-8, which displays columns B through F.
14. On your own, place an identical line of equal signs across cells A5 through G5.
15. Key your identification line at cell A22.
16. Save the worksheet as PRAC10C.
17. Print the wide worksheet.

Decorative borders are Repeat Characters used to visually separate the parts of the worksheet.

Click on cell A2, roll the mouse to the control panel, and click on **C**opy. Then click the button to complete the **Copy what?** range.

Click on cell B2, drag the mouse to cell G2, and then release the button.

Click the mouse button to end the **To where?** range.

```
F1:                                                           READY

      B         C              D              E       F        ◄
 1           CUSTOMER ACCOUNT BALANCES                         ►
 2  =========================================================  ♦
 3           ACCOUNT                     PREVIOUS BALANCE
 4           NUMBER      CUSTOMER NAME   BALANCE  CHANGE       ?
 5  =========================================================
 6         456-22-8874  Williams, Richard Mrs.  55.86   -10.64
 7         656-85-9114  Tipton, Gladys          34.4     70.93
 8         551-34-2782  Mendez, Oscar           12.5      -35
 9         461-82-4645  Richardson, Luetta Ms.  3.66       0
10         405-86-3622  Anderson, Brett        450.32   106.93
11         386-42-6890  Crowder, Tom            53.78      0
12         312-86-2448  Isobe, Reiko           112.65   -43.23
13         865-44-9074  Tramplin, Belinda Mrs. 371.55  -126.19
14         566-28-7671  Johnson, Elliott Mrs.   68.99     -53
15         389-65-4430  Johnson, Robin          37.98      0
16                                             --------------
17  TOTAL                         TOTAL       1201.69   -90.2
18  AVERAGE                       AVERAGE      120.169   -9.02
19  MINIMUM                       MINIMUM        3.66  -126.19
20  MAXIMUM                       MAXIMUM      450.32   106.93
                                                     NUM CAPS
```

Figure 10-8
Repeat Characters placed across rows.

NEW COMMANDS AND KEYS

/ Copy. Copies data from one place to another, leaving the data in both places.

F4. The function key used to place dollar signs in an absolute cell address.

\. The key used to begin repeat characters.

FILES CREATED IN THIS SECTION

PRAC10A

PRAC10B

PRAC10C

ACT101A

ACT101B

ACT102

ACT103

ACTIVITIES

(Template File: ACT101TP)

ACTIVITY 10-1

```
            A              B        C          D          E
1.    DESCRIPTION        JULY    AUGUST   SEPTEMBER    TOTAL
2.
3.    RECEIPTS
4.       SALES           4500     6800      6800
5.       SERVICE         6200     8500      8000
6.       TOTAL
7.
8.    PAYMENTS
9.       PRODUCT
10.      SALARIES        2000
11.      RENT            1000
12.      INSURANCE        123                130
13.      UTILITIES        120
14.      SUPPLIES          55       90        90
15.      TOTAL
16.
```

Key the worksheet shown above. The column heading DESCRIPTION is centered, and column A is widened to 15. All other column headings are right aligned. Press the space bar to indent the DESCRIPTION items where shown.

1. Key an @SUM function at B6 to total July Sales and Service receipts. Key an @SUM function at B15 to total the July payments. Then copy the functions to C6 through D6 and C15 through D15.

2. Key a formula for the Product payment amounts (B9-D9), which are 50% of the sales figure for their respective months. To do this, key a formula at B9 that will multiply the sales amount for July (B4) by .5 (50%). Copy the formula to cells C9 and D9.

3. Copy the fixed amounts. Salaries, rent, and utilities will remain about the same. Copy these amounts in column B into columns C and D.

4. Copy the Insurance amount at B12 to C12.

5. Total each receipt and each payment for the 3-month period. At E4 key a function to total cells B4, C4, and D4. Copy the function to cells E5 through E15.

6. Delete the unwanted zeros in cells E7 and E8 with **DELETE** or Range Erase.

7. Save the sheet as ACT101A.

8. The worksheet needs some headings. Insert four rows at row 1. (The range is rows 1 to 4.) Key the following headings at A1, A2, and A3:

    ```
    QUALITY OFFICE SUPPLIES
    ESTIMATED RECEIPTS AND PAYMENTS
    FOR THE QUARTER ENDED SEPTEMBER 199-
    ```

9. Place quotes (") across row 4. At A4 use Repeat Characters and then copy it across to B4 through E4.

10. Insert a new row at row 10. Then use Repeat Characters to place hyphens at B10, above the total figure. Copy this to C10 through E10. Repeat these steps at row 20.

11. Globally format for comma with 2 decimal places.

12. Globally widen cells to 12 places.

13. Use Range Format Currency to place dollar signs for all figures in Rows 8, 11, 14, and 21.

14. Save the worksheet as ACT101B. Print it. Keep it on your screen to use in the next activity.

Retrieve ACT101B.

ACTIVITY 10-2

1. Goto A23. Key the label: EST. INCOME

2. At B23 key a formula to find the difference between Total Receipts and Total Payments. Point to the cells (B11 and B21) as you key the formula. Copy the formula to cells C23 through E23. Format the cells for currency.

3. Use Repeat Characters to place equal signs (=) from A24 to E24.

4. Use Titles to freeze both column A and rows 1 through 5. Place the pointer at B6 to begin the command for Titles Both.

5. Key at F8 key a formula that will calculate the percent of change from the beginning of the quarter (July) to the end of the quarter (September). To find the percent of change, subtract the July figure (B8) *from* the September figure (D8) and then divide by the July figure (B8). Point to the cells as you build the formula. Use parentheses around the subtraction part of the formula so it will be performed before the division. (The result of the calculation at F8 is .51.)

6. Copy the formula at F8 to cells F9 through F23. Erase any cells that should be blank but instead display 0 or ERR. Be careful not to erase numeric cells that contain zero as a legitimate percentage.

7. Clear the Titles. Then format column F with the Range Format Percent command, using 2 decimal places.

8. Key at F5 a right-aligned label: % CHANGE.

9. Tidy the worksheet by copying from column E quotes, rulings, and equal signs to wherever needed in column F.

10. Place quotes from A6 to F6 using Repeat Character and the copy command.

11. Save the worksheet as ACT102.

12. Print the wide worksheet and then erase it.

ACTIVITY 10-3

1. Retrieve the ACT81 worksheet.
2. Set Titles for column A.
3. Add the following product data to the worksheet. Enter the percents as *decimals*. Right align the Product #'s.

    ```
    Product #              TY5576      ST210814    LM31262
    Current Price          15.88       29.99       23.50
    % of Increase          3.5%        4.15%       2.8%
    Est. Number of Sales   650         500         600
    ```

4. Format G7 through I7 for percent format. Format G10 through I10 for fixed format, no decimals.
5. Compute the New Price and the Estimated Sales Amount for each product by copying the formulas at F8 and F11.
6. Clear titles so you can key in column A. At cell A13 key the label: Total Estimated Sales. At cell B13 key a function that will add all the Estimated Sales Amounts.
7. Insert a new row at row 12.
8. At cell A12 key the label: % of Estimated Total Sales. At cell B12 key a formula that will divide the Estimated Sales Amount at B11 by the Total Estimated Sales figure at B14. Make cell B14 an *absolute* cell address.
9. Copy the % of Estimated Total Sales formula at B12 across the row. Cell B14 should copy absolute.
10. Format cells as needed.
11. Using **R**epeat Characters, place decorative lines in rows 3, 5, 9, 13, and 15.
12. Save the worksheet as ACT103.
13. Print the worksheet.

LESSON 11

Sorting

OBJECTIVES

- Recognize that a spreadsheet is a database
- Distinguish between ascending and descending order
- Set a primary and a secondary sort range
- Sort alphabetically and numerically
- Reset data sort settings

Estimated Time: 35 minutes

VOCABULARY

Ascending order   Field name   Secondary-Key
Data-Range   Primary-Key   Sort
Descending order   Record   Sort order
Field

1-2-3 AS A DATABASE

A database is software that enables a person to enter data records, arrange them alphabetically or numerically, select only records which meet a particular criteria, and print the data in the desired form. Because you can perform all of these functions in 1-2-3, many people use 1-2-3 as both a spreadsheet and a database. You have already learned to enter records and print. In this lesson you will learn the database function of sorting records, and in the next lesson you will learn to select records.

Most worksheets are set up so that a *row* is a **record** and a *column* is a **field**. Figure 11-1 shows part of the PRAC10A worksheet. Each row, separated by a horizontal line, contains a record of data about a customer.

In most spreadsheets, a row is a **record** and a column is a **field**.

45.22	456-22-8874	Williams, Richard Mrs.	55.86
105.33	656-85-9114	Tipton, Gladys	34.4
-22.5	551-34-2782	Mendez, Oscar	12.5
3.66	461-82-4645	Richardson, Luetta Ms.	3.66
557.25	405-86-3622	Anderson, Brett	450.32

Figure 11-1
Horizontal rows are usually called **records**.

The first row, data about Mrs. Richard Williams, is a record. The second row, data about Gladys Tipton, is a record, and so on. Always include entire records (rows) in the range of data to be sorted to avoid separating fields of data from their appropriate records. For example, it would be an error to give Mrs. Williams' account number to Oscar Mendez through incorrect sorting.

Figure 11-2 also displays part of the PRAC10A worksheet. This time it is shown divided by vertical lines into *fields*, which are *specific items* of data such as account numbers, names, and account balances. Each column heading is a **field name**.

> **NOTE**
>
> Always include entire records (rows) in the range of data to be sorted.

ACCOUNT BALANCE	ACCOUNT NUMBER	CUSTOMER NAME	PREVIOUS BALANCE
45.22	456-22-8874	Williams, Richard Mrs.	55.86
105.33	656-85-9114	Tipton, Gladys	34.4
-22.5	551-34-2782	Mendez, Oscar	12.5
3.66	461-82-4645	Richardson, Luetta Ms.	3.66
557.25	405-86-3622	Anderson, Brett	450.32

Figure 11-2
Vertical columns are usually called **fields**.

When you sort a worksheet, you select the field you want to **sort**, or arrange in order. For example, if the part of a worksheet shown in Figure 11-2 were sorted in alphabetical order on the Customer Name field, Brett Anderson's record would be first, and Mrs. Richard Williams' record would be last.

QUICK QUESTIONS

1. Why is 1-2-3 like a database?
2. What part of a worksheet usually contains one record?
3. What part of a worksheet can usually be considered a field?
4. What parts of records should be included in the range of data to be sorted?
5. What part of the worksheet is a field name?

SORTING

Because it simplifies data entry, records are often entered into a spreadsheet in random order. Rearranging the records into alphabetic or numeric order, however, can make the data easier to read and analyze. You can use the **Data Sort** command to arrange records in alphabetic or numeric order.

The Data Sort command is used to arrange records in alphabetic or numeric order.

DATA RANGE

When sorting, you must first set the **Data-Range**, the range of records to be sorted. Include all of the records in the database, but do *not* include headings, totals, or decorative lines in a sort range. The Data-Range must include all fields of all records you wish to sort.

Include all records, but do not include headings and totals in the Data-Range.

SORT KEY

After the Data-Range has been set, you can select the **Primary-Key** (the field on which the records will be sorted). If some of the entries in the Primary-Key field are identical, you can sort the records further using an additional sort, the **Secondary-Key**. *Release 3.x has additional sort keys defined by Extra-Sort.*

SORT ORDER

After the sort key is selected, 1-2-3 asks you for the **sort order**. You may choose ascending or descending order. **Ascending** order is the normal sort order, with letters going from A to Z and numbers from lowest to highest. **Descending** order arranges letters from Z to A and numbers from highest to lowest. Descending is the default sort order; use it when you want to see the largest values first.

Ascending order has letters going from A to Z and numbers from lowest to highest.

PERFORM THE SORT

Finally, the command **Go** will perform the sort.

QUICK QUESTIONS

1. Why are records often arranged in alphabetic or numeric order?
2. What command do you use to arrange records in order?
3. What is the Data-Range?
4. What worksheet items should *not* be included in the Data-Range?
5. What is the Primary-Key?
6. What is the Secondary-Key?
7. Which sort order goes from Z to A and largest number to smallest?
8. When should you use the descending order option?
9. What subcommand perfoms the sort?

EXERCISE 11-1

1. Retrieve the PRAC10A worksheet.

The first sort will arrange the records in ascending order on the Customer Name field. Remember, entire records must be included in the data-range.

2. Go to the beginning of the range of records to be sorted (cell A6).
3. [A6] / **D**ata **S**ort
4. [A6] **D**ata-**R**ange

Move the mouse to the control panel, click on Data, Sort and then release the button.

The next step is often done incorrectly. Be sure your data range includes **all fields** of **all records**, but do not include headings, totals, or decorative lines. The Data-Range for this exercise is A6..E15.

5. [A6] **.** to anchor the beginning of the data-range
6. [E15] **ENTER** to end the data-range, which includes all records on the worksheet
7. [A6] **P**rimary-**K**ey

Click on **D**ata-**R**ange.

Click on cell A6, drag the mouse to cell E15, and then release the button.

Click the mouse button to end the Data-Range, which includes all records on the worksheet.

Click on **P**rimary-**K**ey.

144 LESSON 11 SORTING

8. Since you are sorting on the Customer Name field in column D, point to column D in any record and then press **ENTER** to set it as the primary sort key.

A new option appears at the right on the control panel (**Sort order A or D**), as shown in Figure 11-3. This sort will be in ascending order.

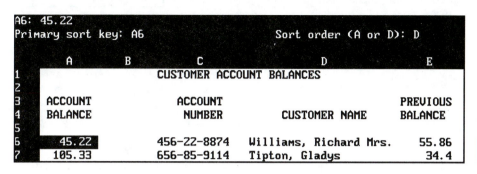

Since you are sorting on the Customer Name field in column D, click on column D in any record and then click the mouse button to set it as the primary sort key.

Figure 11-3
The Sort Order option.

9. Key **ENTER** to set the Sort Order to **ascending**.

10. Key **G**o to perform the sort.

Key and then click the mouse button to set the Sort Order to **ascending**.

Click on Go to perform the sort.

Verify that the customer names are arranged in order from Anderson to Williams, as shown in Figure 11-4. If the records are not arranged correctly, do the sort again.

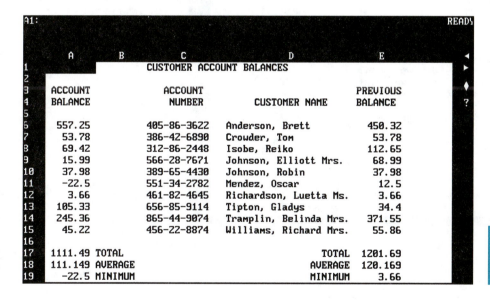

Figure 11-4
The Customer Name field arranged in ascending order.

The next sort on the PRAC10A worksheet will arrange the Account Number field in ascending order.

1. [A6] / **D**ata **S**ort **D**ata-Range

The previous Data-Range should reappear (A6..E15). When using the previous Data-Range for the following exercises, it is not necessary to select Data-Range until you want to change the range. (If for some reason the data-range needs to be reset, press **ESC**, anchor the range at A6, and then go to E15 as the end of the range.)

EXERCISE 11-2

Move the mouse to the control panel and then click on Data, Sort, Data-Range.

2. Press **ENTER** to accept the current data-range.

3. Key **P**rimary-Key

4. Point to column C in any record, the Account Number field, and then press **ENTER** to set it as the primary sort key.

The sort order is already set for A.

5. Key **ENTER** to accept ascending sort order.

6. Key **G**o.

The account numbers should be arranged in numeric order, from the lowest to the highest. Check your work against Figure 11-5.

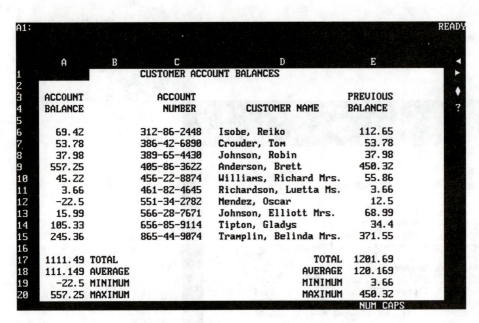

To reset a Data-Range, press Esc and then set the new range.

Click the button to accept the current data-range.

Click on Primary-Key.

Click on column C, the Account Number field, in any record. Then click the button to set it as the primary sort key.

Click the button to accept ascending sort order.

Click on Go.

Figure 11-5
The Account Number field arranged in ascending order.

Sometimes it is helpful to sort so that the largest values are displayed first. For this exercise, assume the store owner is very interested in how much money is owed her by her customers. The customers who owe the most should be at the top of the list. Sort the Account Balance column in descending order so the largest balances are shown first.

1. [A6] / **D**ata **S**ort (The previous Data-Range, A6..E15, is still in effect.)

2. [A6] **P**rimary-Key

▶ **EXERCISE 11-3**

Move the mouse to the control panel and click on Data, Sort. (The previous Data-Range, A6..E15, is still in effect.)

Click on Primary-Key.

3. Point to column A in any record to select the Account Balance field. Then press **ENTER**.

4. Key **d** **ENTER** for descending order.

5. Key **G**o to sort.

Click on column A in any record to select the Account Balance field. Then click the button.

Check to see if the sorting is correct, with the balances in largest to smallest order.

6. On your own, sort in descending order the Previous Balance field.

7. Save the worksheet as PRAC11A.

8. Print the worksheet.

Key **d** for descending order and then click the button.

Click on Go to sort.

SECONDARY SORT

The **Secondary-Key** allows you to sort on two fields, sometimes called a "sort within a sort." The Primary sort key determines the first field that will be arranged in order. Then, the records *within* that sort can be arranged on a second field using the Secondary sort key. In other words, the entire secondary sort field will not be arranged in order; only the records that are alike in the primary sort field will be arranged in order. This is helpful for data analysis when the primary sort field contains some identical data.

NOTE

Use a secondary sort when the primary sort field contains some identical data.

▶ **EXERCISE 11-4**

Edit the PRAC11A worksheet and then sort it in several ways.

1. Insert a new column at A using the Worksheet Insert Column command. (The new column will be column A.)

2. Key the following data:

   [A3] DAYS
   [A4] OVERDUE

   Use the Range Label command to right align the labels at A3 and A4.

   [A6] 30
   [A7] 60
   [A8] 0
   [A9] 30
   [A10] 90
   [A11] 30
   [A12] 60
   [A13] 90
   [A14] 30
   [A15] 30

The store owner wants to analyze the number of days customers are overdue and how much is owed by those who are overdue. First, sort the worksheet in descending order on the Days Overdue field.

3. [A6] At the first record, press / **D**ata **S**ort **D**ata-Range.

Move the mouse to the control panel and click on Data, Sort, Data-Range.

4. Press **ESC** to cancel the previous Data-Range.

5. [A6] Press **.** to anchor the Data-Range.

6. [F15] Press **ENTER** to end the Data-Range at the last record.

7. Key **P**rimary-**K**ey

8. Point to a column A in any record to select the Days Overdue field. Press **ENTER**.

9. Key **d** for descending order. Press **ENTER**.

10. Key **G**o.

Analyze the sort (see Figure 11-6). The Days Overdue are listed from greatest to least, but there are some duplicate entries. Two customers are 90 days overdue, two customers are 60 days overdue, and five customers are 30 days overdue. The information presented by the worksheet would be easier to analyze if the Account Balances were arranged in order within the Days Overdue sort. For example, all of the 90 days overdue records should also be arranged on the Account Balance field.

Click the **right** mouse button to cancel the previous Data-Range.

Click on cell A6, drag the mouse to cell F15, and then release the button.

Click the button to end the Data-Range.

Click on Primary-Key.

Click on column A in any record to select the Days Overdue field. Then click the mouse button.

Key **d** for descending order. Click the mouse button.

Click on Go.

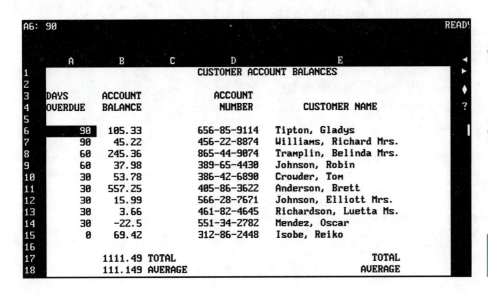

Figure 11-6
The worksheet after the primary sort.

Set a Secondary-Key on the Account Balance field.

11. Key **/ D**ata **S**ort.

Since the data range and primary key are still set correctly from the previous sort, it is not necessary to select Data-Range or Primary-Key.

12. Key **S**econdary-Key.

13. Point to column B, the Account Balance field. Press **ENTER**.

Move the mouse to the control panel and click on Data, Sort.

Click on Secondary-Key.

Click on column B, the secondary sort field. Then click the mouse button.

14. Press **ENTER** to accept descending order.

15. Key **G**o.

Click the mouse button to accept descending order.

Click on Go.

Check the result of sorting on two fields (see Figure 11-7). The records are sorted on the Days Overdue field, and within that field the records are sorted according to their Account Balances. For example, the Account Balances in the 30 Days Overdue field are in numeric order. The owner can easily relate the days overdue with the amount still owed by customers.

Save the worksheet as PRAC11B. Keep it on your screen.

Figure 11-7
The worksheet after the secondary sort.

RESET

After you have sorted a worksheet, you may wish to use the **Data Sort Reset** command. This clears the Data-Range and the primary and secondary sort key settings from the previous sort.

> **NOTE**
>
> The Data Sort Reset command clears the Data-Range and sort keys.

QUICK QUESTIONS

1. How can you simplify data analysis when you sort on a field that has several records with identical data in the sorted column?

2. What command do you use to clear all data sort settings?

Clear the previous Data-Range and sort keys.

1. [A7] / **D**ata **S**ort **R**eset **Q**uit

All data sort settings are cleared. Make a new sort using Primary and Secondary keys.

2. On your own, make Days Overdue the primary sort field in ascending order, and Previous Balance the secondary sort field in descending order. Do not forget to set the data range as all records and fields in the database, from A6 to F15.

3. Save the worksheet as PRAC11C.

4. Print the worksheet and then erase it.

>
> **EXERCISE 11-5**
>
> Move the mouse to the control panel and click on Data, Sort, Reset, Quit.

NEW COMMANDS AND KEYS

/ Data Sort. Arranges records in alphabetic or numeric order.

/ Data Sort Reset. Clears the Data-Range and the primary and secondary sort key settings from the previous sort.

FILES CREATED IN THIS LESSON

PRAC11A
PRAC11B
PRAC11C
ACT111
ACT111A
ACT111B
ACT111C
ACT111D
ACT112A
ACT112B
ACT112C
ACT113A
ACT113B
ACT113C
CTP11A
CTP11B
CTP11C

150   **LESSON 11**   SORTING

ACTIVITIES

(Template File: ACT111TP)

ACTIVITY 11-1

```
              A              B          C      D       E     F
 1.  COLLEGE EXAM, INC
 2.  EXAMINEES
 3.  SATURDAY, MAY 8, 1993
 4.  ***************************************************
 5.  NAME            SOCSEC NO    SEX   VERBAL  MATH
 6.  ***************************************************
 7.  Crawford, Frank  454-88-5471  M     548    547
 8.  Velez, Amelia    576-36-1873  F     457    483
 9.  Tampps, LeGrand  312-74-7821  M     463    588
10.  Huff, Elaine     438-10-2372  F     548    547
11.  Runyan, Grace    610-29-8631  F     686    650
12.  Morales, Mario   357-72-5832  M     548    647
13.  Peterson, Kathy  574-20-3558  F     457    483
14.  Bancroft, Wayne  411-95-3264  M     463    407
15.  Forey, Harold    278-71-2239  M     575    516
16.  Toney, James     638-24-6684  M     548    483
17.  Honey, Ryan      584-33-4287  M     575    547
18.  Capps, Sandy     721-56-7328  F     457    461
19.  Prince, Amy      681-63-9005  F     389    588
```

Key the worksheet shown above. Align labels as shown and widen columns as needed. Use repeat characters. After saving the worksheet as ACT111, complete the sorting described below.

1. Sort the worksheet in ascending order on the Name field. Save the sorted worksheet as ACT111A. Print it.

2. Sort the worksheet on the Sex field as a primary sort (ascending) and the Name field as a secondary sort (ascending). Save the sorted worksheet as ACT111B. Print it.

3. Sort the worksheet with Verbal as the primary sort (descending) and Name as the secondary sort (ascending). Save the sorted worksheet as ACT111C. Print it.

4. Sort the math scores from highest to lowest; alphabetize within the math score groupings. Save the sorted worksheet as ACT111D. Print it.

ACTIVITY 11-2

1. Retrieve the PRAC7B worksheet. Set a global column width of 9.

2. Insert a new column at column B. Key the following data in the new column B:

   [B3] GRADE   (right aligned)
   [B5] 10
   [B6] 11
   [B7] 9
   [B8] 10
   [B9] 12
   [B10] 12
   [B11] 10
   [B12] 9
   [B13] 12
   [B14] 11

3. Sort the worksheet alphabetically. Save the sorted worksheet as ACT112A. Print it.

4. Sort the worksheet on the Grade field with grade 12 first and grade 9 last. Save the sorted worksheet as ACT112B. Print it.

5. Sort the worksheet on the GRADE field, lowest to highest, but arrange the students alphabetically as a secondary sort. Save the sorted worksheet as ACT112C. Print it.

ACTIVITY 11-3

1. Retrieve the ACT92 worksheet. Use *ascending* order for all sorts.
2. Sort the worksheet on the Description field. Save the worksheet as ACT113A. Print it.
3. Sort the worksheet on the Labor Type field. Save the worksheet as ACT113B. Print it.
4. Sort the worksheet on the Labor Type field as a primary sort and on the Operation field as a secondary sort. Save the worksheet as ACT113C. Print it.

CRITICAL THINKING PROJECT 11

Retrieve the CTP3 worksheet. If it is not on your disk, go to Critical Thinking Project C in Lesson 3 and complete the initial worksheet before continuing.

The club had a fund raising drive, and you as treasurer are to make entries for each member in the following categories (fields): number of merchandise items taken, total owed for the items, amount paid, and amount still owed. The items all sold for $5, nontaxable.

Make appropriate columns with column headings for the data. You make up the number of items taken and the amount paid by each member. After you use a formula or function to determine the total owed and the amount still owed, copy the formula or function down the column. Total the numeric columns.

It is your responsibiity to analyze the worksheet to determine who still owes money and how much, who sold the most items, and so forth. Show this information more clearly by sorting the worksheet.

Complete three meaningful sorts of the worksheet, at least two of them with a secondary sort. At the bottom of each sorted worksheet, key an explanation of the sort you made. Print the sorts and turn in. Save the sorted files as CTP11A, CTP11B, and CTP11C.

LESSON 12

Data Queries and Data Fill

OBJECTIVES

- Query to edit records
- Use wildcards for unknown data
- Query to delete records
- Query to extract records
- Number records with data fill

Estimated Time: 60 minutes.

VOCABULARY

Criteria
Criterion
Criteria range
Input range
Output range
Query
Wildcards

DATA QUERY

As you discovered in Lesson 11, spreadsheets can be used for database operations, in addition to worksheet calculations. You used the Data Sort command to arrange records for more effective data analysis by sorting on fields. Now you will use the **Data Query** commands to select certain records by field so they can be edited or displayed separately from the rest of the database. When you are performing database functions on a worksheet, the worksheet is called a database.

When you inquire whether particular records exist in a database, you are performing a **query** (question). Queries are very helpful for large databases, because it would require much time and patience to manually search through many records. To complete a query, you must set a criteria and input range, and sometimes an output range.

Data queries are important when a database has too many records to readily view.

INPUT RANGE

The **input range**, set with the **Data Query Input** command, specifies the range of records to be queried, just as the Data-Range command specified the range of records to be sorted in Lesson 11. Include complete records *as well as field names* (column headings) in the input range. Do *not* include main headings, total lines, blank lines, or decorative lines.

The Data Query input range includes all of the records in the database and the field names.

OUTPUT RANGE

Where 1-2-3 will place copies of the records selected by a query is determined by the **output range**, which you set with the **Data Query Output** command. The output range is usually to the right of or below the database.

The first row of the output range contains the field names of the data you wish to see as a result of the query. The field names must be spelled as they are in the input range, but they can be in any order. The answer to the query will be placed right below the field names. An output range is used only with the Data Query Extract and Data Query Unique commands.

The output range includes the desired input range fields arranged in any order.

CRITERIA RANGE

The **Data Query Criteria** command is used to specify the search fields and the search criteria. The first row of the **criteria range** must contain the input range field names that 1-2-3 is to search. The criteria you wish to use for selecting records is keyed below the field names. The criteria values used must be preceded by an apostrophe. Like the output range, the criteria range is usually to the right of or below the database.

The criteria range includes the names of fields to be searched and the criteria to be used.

PREPARING A DATABASE FOR QUERY

Before you begin a query, check to see that the following requirements have been met:

- The first row of the database must contain field names in adjacent columns.
- Duplicate field names are not allowed.
- The second and following rows must contain database records.
- Blank rows or decorative lines between field names and the records are not allowed.
- The entries in each field must be all labels or all values.

> **NOTE**
>
> Blank rows or decorative lines between field names and the records in a database are not allowed.

DATA QUERY STEPS

As you are making data queries, you may wish to refer to Figure 12-1, which outlines each step of the query process.

1.	Save the worksheet.	This will protect your database in case you overwrite it with query data.
2.	Prepare the criteria.	Copy the field names from the top row of the input range to a blank area of the worksheet. Key the search criteria in the row(s) below the field names.
3.	If using **Q**uery **E**xtract or **Q**uery **U**nique, prepare the output.	Copy the desired field names from the top row of the input range to a new blank area of the worksheet.
4.	/ **D**ata **Q**uery	Start the query command.
5.	Input range.	Specify the input range, which includes the field names and all records to be searched.
6.	Criteria range.	Specify the criteria range, which is the criteria field name(s) and search condition(s).
7.	If you are using **Q**uery **E**xtract or **Q**uery **U**nique, select **O**utput **R**ange.	Specify the output range, which is the output field name(s) and blank rows in which 1-2-3 will place the result of the query.
8.	Select the query operation.	Select **D**elete, **E**xtract, **F**ind, or **U**nique.
9.	**Q**uit.	Return to Ready mode.

Figure 12-1
Steps to perform a query.

QUICK QUESTIONS

1. What is a database query?
2. What is specified by the input range?
3. What is determined by the output range?
4. What must appear on the first row of the output range?
5. Which two data query commands require an output range?

    a.

    b.

6. What is the purpose of the Data Query Criteria command?
7. What must appear on the first row of the criteria range?
8. Can you include blank rows or decorative lines in a database that will be queried?

▶ **EXERCISE 12-1**

1. Retrieve the ACT111A worksheet. (The Name field should be arranged in ascending order.)

Although saving a database before querying it is a good idea, we will not follow that procedure in the following exercises because each database is already saved on your disk. It is necessary, however, to remove the decorative line between the field names and the first record in the database.

2. [A6] / **W**orksheet **D**elete **R**ow `ENTER`

Now the worksheet is ready to be used as a database and to be queried.

N O T E

To protect your database, save it on your disk before beginning a query.

QUERY FIND

The **Data Query Find** command locates records in the input range that match your specified **criteria**. You should use this command when you are searching for records to be edited.

To use Query Find, specify an input range and a criteria range. Then key / Data Query Find. 1-2-3 will highlight the first record in the input range that matches the criteria. Use the cursor keys described in Figure 12-2 to move among the matching records. If there are no matching records, 1-2-3 will beep.

N O T E

The Data Query Find command locates records in the input range that match the condition in the criteria range. 1-2-3 will highlight matching records and beep when there are no matching records.

↑ or ↓	Moves the pointer to other matching records. 1-2-3 beeps if there are no matching records.
→ or ←	Moves the pointer among fields in the current matching record.
Edit (F2)	Enables you to edit the current matching record. Press Enter to save the changes and continue with Query Find, or press Esc to cancel changes and continue with Query Find.
Enter or Esc	Ends Query Find and returns to the Query menu.
Home or End	Moves the pointer to the first or last matching record.
Query (F7)	Ends Query Find and returns to Ready mode.

Figure 12-2
Moving among matching records in a Find query.

QUICK QUESTIONS

1. Which command do you use to locate records in the input range that match your specified criteria?
2. When you are doing a Find query, how will you know which record matches the search criteria?
3. When you are doing a Find query, how will you know that there are no more matching records?
4. Which key do you press to move to the next matching record in a Find query?
5. When you are doing a Find query, what key do you press to move the pointer among fields in the current matching record?
6. Which keys do you use to end the Find query and return to the Query menu?

EXERCISE 12-2

Use the Find query to search for all records that have a verbal score greater than 500 in the ACT111A database. Count the records that meet the criteria.

PREPARE THE CRITERIA. First, copy the field name(s) to the first row of the criteria range (a blank area of the worksheet). After the database field names are placed, key the query condition right below the name of the field to be queried. (Leave the field names in the criteria range for later queries.)

Copy all field names in cells A5 through E5 to cells G5 through K5 (the first row of the criteria range).

1. [A5] / **C**opy
2. [A5] **(.)** to anchor the range if you are using Release 2.2.
3. Point to E5 and key **ENTER** to complete the **Copy what?** range.
4. Point to G5 and key **ENTER** to complete the **To where?** range.
5. Check your database screen against Figure 12-3.

Move the mouse to the control panel and click on Copy.

Click on cell A5, drag the mouse to cell E5, and release the button. Then click the button to complete the **Copy what?** range.

Click on cell G5 and then click the button to complete the **To where?** range.

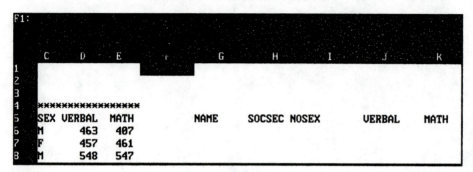

Figure 12-3
The first row of the criteria range contains field names.

Next, key the **criterion** 1-2-3 should use to find the desired record(s). The criterion must be placed in the second row of the criteria range (row 6) under the appropriate field name. The criterion must begin with an apostrophe.

Key the search criterion at cell J6, under the appropriate field name (column heading), **Verbal**. The search criterion is **greater than 500**. Precede the greater-than sign (>) with quotes or an apostrophe, (see the contents line in Figure 12-4).

6. [J6] **(')** **(>)** 500 **ENTER**

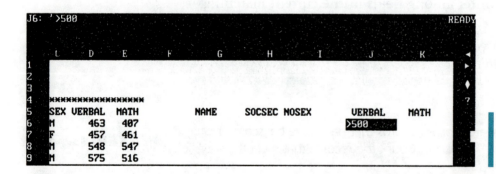

Figure 12-4
The Contents line shows that **' > 500** is the criterion entered at cell J6.

Now that the criteria has been prepared, begin the Data Query commands.

INPUT RANGE. Specify the input range, which is all of the records in the database as well as the field names (column headings).

7. [A5] / **D**ata **Q**uery **I**nput **(.)** (anchors the input range)

Move the mouse to the control panel and click on Data, Query, Input.

8. [E18] **ENTER** to end the input range

9. Check your database screen against Figure 12-5.

Click on cell A5, drag the mouse to cell E18, and then release the button. Click the button to end the input range.

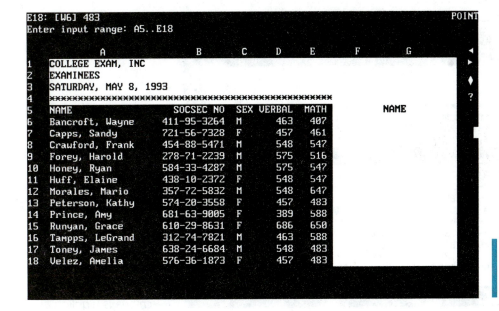

Figure 12-5
The input range consists of field names and records.

CRITERIA RANGE. The criteria range has been prepared with the field names and criteria. Now it is necessary to tell 1-2-3 where the criteria range is. Select the Criteria subcommand on the Query menu and then set the range.

10. Key **C**riteria (selects the Criteria subcommand).

11. Point to cell J5, the first cell of the criteria range. Key **.**.

12. Point to cell J6, the last cell of the criteria range. Check your screen against Figure 12-6. Key **ENTER**.

Click on Criteria to select the subcommand.

Click on cell J5, drag the mouse to cell J6, and then release the button.

Click the button to end the criteria range.

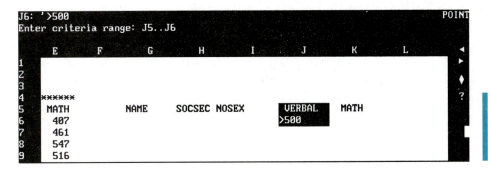

Figure 12-6
The criteria range consists of the field name(s) and the criteria to be used in the query.

BEGIN THE QUERY. Both the input and criteria ranges have been set. The query subcommand Find will begin the query.

13. Key **F**ind (subcommand that begins the query)

Click on the subcommand Find to begin the query.

As shown in Figure 12-7, the first record to match the criterion, the Crawford record, is highlighted. His verbal score is 548, which is greater than 500.

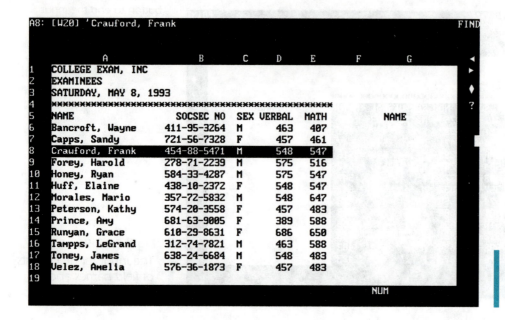

Figure 12-7
After selecting Find, the first record to meet the criteria is highlighted.

14. Key ⬇ repeatedly to search for more matching records.

1-2-3 skips over records that do not meet the criterion and beeps when there are no other matching records.

15. Key F7 to end the search.

16. Save the database as PRAC12A. Use it for the following exercise.

To move to the next record that matches the criterion, press ⬇.

SEARCH FOR LABELS

When searching for labels, you must key them exactly as they appear in the database. If you are not certain of the spelling, **wildcards** can be used for unknown parts of a label. Use ? for single unknown characters, and use * for unknown characters to the end of the label. Preceding a label with ~ will find all occurrences except that particular label.

The wildcards ? and * can be used to search for unknown parts of data.

QUICK QUESTIONS

1. What should appear on the first row of the criteria range?
2. What should appear on the second row of the criteria range?
3. What two items appear in the input range?
4. What character must precede a search criterion such as < than 300?
5. Which subcommand will begin the query?
6. How must labels be keyed for query?
7. If you know that a name begins with **Mc**, what wildcard can you use with **Mc** to complete the query?

You need to correct the spelling of Amy Price's name, but you are not sure how it was misspelled. What you do know is that her name was keyed beginning with **Pri**. Use the * wildcard for **unknown** or **remaining** characters in a criterion.

▶ EXERCISE 12-3

PREPARE THE CRITERIA. First, correct the criterion for this search.

1. Point to cell G6.
2. [G6] Pri* **ENTER**

Click on cell G6.

INPUT RANGE. The previous input range is correct so you do not need to make any changes here.

Move the mouse to the control panel and click on Data, Query, Criteria.

CRITERIA RANGE. Next, you need to change the criteria range from the Verbal field to the Name field, so the Criteria range must be reset to cells G5..G6.

3. Key / **D**ata **Q**uery **C**riteria.
4. Press **ESC** to cancel the previous criteria range.

Click the **right** mouse button to cancel the previous criteria range.

5. Point to cell G5. Key **.**.
6. Point to G6. Key **ENTER**.

BEGIN THE QUERY. Since the Query menu is already on the control panel, select the subcommand Find to begin the query.

Click on cell G5, drag the mouse to cell G6, and then release the mouse button.

7. Key **F**ind.

1-2-3 stops at the first matching record, shown in Figure 12-8. It is the record you want to edit by changing **Prince** to **Price**.

Click the mouse button.

Click on Find.

LESSON 12 DATA QUERIES AND DATA FILL   **163**

```
A14: [W20] 'Prince, Amy

           A              B        C    D      E         F      G
1   COLLEGE EXAM, INC
2   EXAMINEES
3   SATURDAY, MAY 8, 1993
4   xxxxxxxxxxxxxxxxxxxxxxxxxxxxxxxxxxxxxxxxxxx
5   NAME             SOCSEC NO   SEX  VERBAL  MATH       NAME
6   Bancroft, Wayne  411-95-3264  M    463    407        Pri*
7   Capps, Sandy     721-56-7328  F    457    461
8   Crawford, Frank  454-88-5471  M    548    547
9   Forey, Harold    278-71-2239  M    575    516
10  Honey, Ryan      584-33-4287  M    575    547
11  Huff, Elaine     438-10-2372  F    548    547
12  Morales, Mario   357-72-5832  M    548    647
13  Peterson, Kathy  574-20-3558  F    457    483
14  Prince, Amy      681-63-9005  F    389    588
15  Runyan, Grace    610-29-8631  F    676    650
```

Figure 12-8
1-2-3 highlights the first record that matches the criterion placed in cell G6.

8. Key **F2** to edit.

9. Key **←** until the pointer is on the **n** in **Prince**. Press **DELETE**.

10. Key **ENTER** to complete the edit.

11. Key **F7** to end the Find query and exit the Query menu.

12. Save the database as PRAC12A, using Replace. Keep the database on your screen to use in the next exercise.

QUERY DELETE

When you wish to delete records that meet specific criteria, use the **Data Query Delete** command. Be cautious with this command; the records to be deleted are not highlighted in any way for you to view before you verify deletion. 1-2-3 will automatically remove the blank rows caused by the deleted records. Both input and criteria ranges must be set before you use the Query Delete command.

One of the students, Elaine Huff, has moved out of the school district, so her record should be deleted.

PREPARE THE CRITERIA. The criterion will be Huff* in the Name field.

1. [G6] Huff* **ENTER**.

INPUT RANGE. The input range is already set from the last queries, so you do not need to make any changes here.

CRITERIA RANGE. The criteria range is already set for the name field, so no adjustment is needed.

Use the Data Query Delete command to begin the query.

2. Key / **D**ata **Q**uery.

Use the Data Query Delete command to delete records that meet specific criteria.

▶ **EXERCISE 12-4**

Move the mouse to the control panel and then click on Data, Query.

3. Key **D**elete. Key **D**elete again to verify the deletion.
4. Key **Q**uit to end the Query menu.

View the database. The record for Elaine Huff has been deleted.

5. Save the database as PRAC12B. Use the database for the next exercise.

Click on Delete twice, once to delete and again to verify the deletion.

Click on Quit to end the Query menu.

QUERY EXTRACT

At times you may want to copy, or *extract*, data to a remote area of the worksheet where it can be viewed or printed. The **Data Query Extract** command will find the records that meet your stated criteria and copy entire records or specified fields to the output range, maintaining their formats. Query Extract requires three ranges: input, criteria, and output.

NOTE

Use Data Query extract to copy records or parts of records that meet your specified criteria.

QUICK QUESTIONS

1. Which command do you use to delete records that meet a specific criteria?
2. Will 1-2-3 show you the records that will be deleted before deleting records found in a query?
3. Which command do you use to find particular records and copy them to a blank part of the worksheet?
4. Does an extract query copy entire records or just specific fields of data?
5. What three ranges are needed for an Extract query?
    a.
    b.
    c.

Using the PRAC12B database, extract the names of all students who are male and have a math score of less than 500.

▶ **EXERCISE 12-5**

PREPARE THE CRITERIA. The new criteria is **M** for male in the Sex field and **<500** in the Math field. It is necessary to erase the criteria at cell J6 because it is in the criteria range.

1. [I6] **M** →
2. [J6] / **R**ange **E**rase **ENTER** →
3. [K6] ' **<** 500 **ENTER**

PREPARE THE OUTPUT. As with criteria preparation, output must be prepared before using the Query command. To do this, you must copy the field name(s) from the input range that you wish to use for the output range.

For output, you want only the **name** of each student that meets the selection criteria. Copy from cell A5 to cell G9 the field name NAME.

4. [A5] / **C**opy `ENTER`
5. [G9] `ENTER`

INPUT RANGE. The input range is still set from past queries, so no adjustment is needed.

CRITERIA RANGE. Set the new criteria range.

6. [I5] Key / **D**ata **Q**uery **C**riteria.

Move the mouse to the control panel and then click on Data, Query, Criteria.

7. Key `ESC` to cancel the previous criteria range.

Begin the criteria range at cell I5 and end it at cell K6 as shown in Figure 12-9.

Press the **right** mouse button to cancel the previous criteria range.

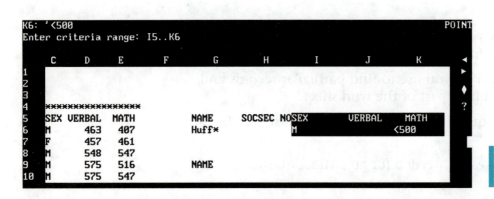

Figure 12-9
The criteria range for the extract is I5..K6.

8. [I5] `.` to anchor the beginning of the criteria range
9. [K6] `ENTER` to end the range

Click on cell I5, drag the mouse to cell K6, and then release the button to set the criteria range.

Click the button to end the range.

OUTPUT RANGE. The first row of the output range is the field name **Name**. The remainder of the output range must be large enough for all records that might meet the selection criteria, because they will be listed vertically below the field name.

Set the output range from cell G9 to cell G15, which is simply an estimate of the number of rows needed. The output range is shown in Figure 12-10. Choose the Output subcommand from the Query menu.

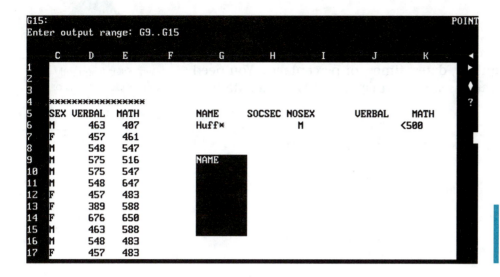

Figure 12-10
The output range for the extract includes G9..G15.

10. Key **O**utput.

11. [G9] **.** to anchor the beginning of the range

12. [G15] **ENTER** to end the range

To begin the extract, use the Extract subcommand and then quit the Query menu.

13. Key **E**xtract.

14. Key **Q**uit.

Two records meet the criteria, Bancroft and Toney, as shown in Figure 12-11.

Click on Output.

Click on cell G9, drag the mouse to cell G15, and then release the button.

Click the mouse button to end the range.

Click on Extract

Click on Quit.

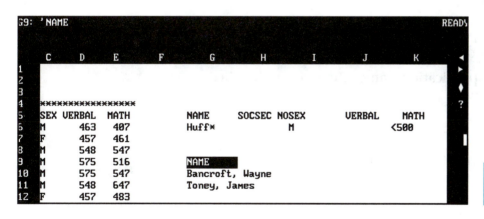

Figure 12-11
The completed extract query.

15. Save the database as PRAC12C. Use the database for the next exercise.

LESSON 12 DATA QUERIES AND DATA FILL **167**

DATA FILL

The **Data Fill** command enters a sequence of values in a range. The values can be numbers, dates, times, or percentages. You need to include the specifications shown in Figure 12-12 for a data fill.

Data Fill is frequently used to number records or place sequential values into a field.

Fill Range	The range to be filled with values.
Start Value	The first value in the fill range (the first number).
Step Value	The increment between each of the values in the fill range. The default value is 1 or the last value entered.
Stop Value	The ending value in the fill range (the last number).

Figure 12-12
Data fill specifications.

QUICK QUESTIONS

1. What is contained in the first row of the output range?
2. How large should you make the output range?
3. Which command enters a sequence of values into a range?
4. Which data fill specification names the ending value in the fill range?
5. Which data fill specification names the beginning value in the fill range?
6. Which data fill specification names the increment of values in the fill range?
7. Which data fill specification names the range to be filled with data fill values?

Insert a new column at column A so the student records can be numbered. Make the column narrow.

EXERCISE 12-6

1. Point to any cell in column A.
2. Key / **W**orksheet **I**nsert **C**olumn **ENTER**.
3. Key / **W**orksheet **C**olumn **S**et-Width **5** **ENTER**.

Use the Data Fill command. The fill range consists of the rows in column A (A6..A17), the start value is 1, the step value is 1, and the stop value is the number of records (12).

4. Key / **D**ata **F**ill.

Move the mouse to the control panel and click on Data, Fill.

5. Point to A6 as the beginning of the fill range. See Figure 12-13.

Click on cell A6, drag the mouse to cell A17, and then release the mouse button.

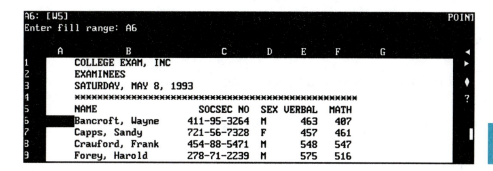

Figure 12-13
Cell A6 is the beginning of the Fill range.

6. [A6] **.**

7. [A17] **ENTER** to end the fill range

8. Key **1** **ENTER** for the start value. See Figure 12-14.

Click the mouse button to end the fill range.

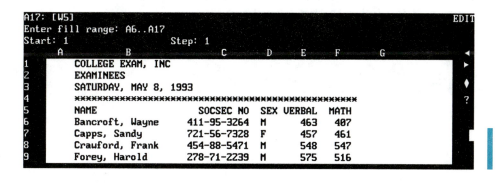

Figure 12-14
Establish the start and step values.

9. Key **ENTER** to accept 1 as the step value.

10. Key 12 **ENTER** as the stop value.

The records are now numbered from 1 to 12.

11. Save the database as PRAC12D. Erase the worksheet.

LESSON 12 DATA QUERIES AND DATA FILL **169**

NEW COMMANDS AND KEYS

/ Data Query Find. Locates records in the input range that match specified criteria. ↑

↑ or ↓. Moves the pointer to other matching records in Query Find.

→ or ←. Moves the pointer among fields in the current matching record in Query Find.

Enter or Esc. Ends the Query Find operation and returns to the Query menu.

Home or End. Moves the pointer to the first or last matching record in Query Find.

F7 (Query). Ends the Query Find operation and returns to Ready mode.

*. Substitute for unknown characters at the end of a label.

?. Substitute for one unknown character in a label.

~. When it precedes a label used as selection criteria, 1-2-3 will find all occurrences except that one.

/ Data Query Delete. Deletes records that meet specific criteria.

/ Data Query Extract. Finds records that meet the stated criteria and copies entire records or specified fields to the output range.

/ Data Fill. Enters a sequence of values in a range.

FILES CREATED IN THIS LESSON

PRAC12A
PRAC12B
PRAC12C
PRAC12D
ACT121A
ACT121B
ACT122
ACT123

ACTIVITIES

(Template File: ACT121TP)

ACTIVITY 12-1

```
           A              B        C          D                E           F
1.   STAMP-IT COMPANY
2.   INVENTORY SHEET
3.   March 31, 199-
4.
5.   STOCK NO         QTY     UNIT    DESCRIPTION       UNIT PRICE    EXTENSION
6.
7.   340-374           15             MOV DATE #1            2.15
8.   340-484           20             MOV DATE #2A           2.15
9.   340-882           13             MOV DATE #3            2.35
10.  340-907            9             MOV DATE #2C           2.35
11.  72-237            16             MOV NUMBER             2.15
12.  72-563            27             MOV PRICE              2.15
13.  75-839            18             DATE AND TIME         19.55
14.  811-172           20             INKED FILE             4.15
15.  811-324           12             INKED AIRMAIL          4.15
16.  811-396           12             INKED COPY             4.15
17.  811-561           21             INKED FOR DEPOSIT ONLY 4.15
18.  811-776            8             INKED CONFIDENTIAL     4.15
```

Key the worksheet shown above. Align labels as shown and widen columns as needed. Column C is empty except for the label UNIT at cell C5. Refer to Figure 12-1 as you query the database.

1. Key the label *EA* in cell C7. Copy the label to cells C8 through C18.

2. Calculate the extension for the first record. To find the extension amount, multiply the quantity times the unit price. Copy the formula to cells F8 through F18.

3. Save the worksheet as ACT121A.

4. To prepare the database for query, delete row 6. Copy all field names to cells I5 through N5 for the criteria range.

5. Use Query Find to change an incorrect stock number, *75-839*, which should be *750-839*. Key '75-839 (preceded by an apostrophe) below the STOCK NO field, in cell I6. Set the input range

LESSON 12 DATA QUERIES AND DATA FILL 171

for cells A5..F17. Set the criteria range for I5..I6. Begin the Find query; use F2 to edit the incorrect cell. Press F7 to end the Find query.

6. STAMP-IT is increasing some prices. Use a Find query to find all records with *MOV DATE** as the Description criteria. Use → to move to the UNIT PRICE field and then add 20¢ to each price. Press ↓ to go to the next selected record until all records that meet the criteria are edited.

7. Save the database as ACT121B and print it. Use it for the next activity.

ACTIVITY 12-2

Use the ACT121B database for the queries below.

1. STAMP-IT is no longer carrying Stock No. 811-396. Use a query to delete the record.
2. It is important to check inventory to be sure STAMP-IT is stocked to meet customer needs. Extract all records that have a quantity less than 15. Include the Stock No. and the Qty. of the extracted records in the output range. Make the output range large enough for at least 6 records.
3. Insert a new column at column A. Narrow the column width. Number the records using Data Fill.
4. Before printing, be sure all columns are as narrow as possible. Print the entire worksheet, columns A through N, using the wide worksheet procedure.
5. Print the output range only.
6. Save the worksheet as ACT122.

ACTIVITY 12-3

1. Retrieve the PRAC7B worksheet.
2. Narrow the columns as much as possible.
3. Erase the label at F3 (TEST 1 TO 4). Move the label at cell F2 to cell F3.
4. Erase the blank row 4.
5. Copy the field names to the criteria range, beginning in cell H3.
6. Query to find and edit a student's name. *Weeks* should be spelled *Weaks*. (Use Weeks* for the criteria.)
7. The instructor has decided to add 3 bonus points to the Test 4 score for everyone who got a score of 90 or more on that test. Use the >= operator to find and edit the appropriate scores.
8. Phil Vance has transferred to another school. Query to delete him from the database.
9. It is the end of the quarter, and all students who increased their score by at least 3% will get a Certificate of Improvement. Use an output range, beginning in cell H7, that contains the extracted students' names and % of increase.
10. Insert a narrow column at column A. Use Data Fill to number the student records.
11. Print the database, columns A through G.
12. Print the range H1 through O18.
13. Save the worksheet as ACT123.

LESSON 13

Graphs

OBJECTIVES

- Explain the purpose of graphs
- Explain data range
- Recognize the elements of a graph
- Create line, bar, multiple bar, stack bar, and pie graphs
- Use graph options
- Name and save graphs
- Print graphs

Estimated Time: 60 minutes.

VOCABULARY

Bar graph	Monochrome monitor	X label
Exploding pie piece	Pie graph	X-axis
First title	PrintGraph	X-axis title
Grid lines	Scale indicator	XY graph
HLCO graph	Second title	Y label
Legend	Shading value	Y-axis
Line graph	Stack bar graph	Y-axis title
Mixed graph		

GRAPHS

The 1-2-3 graph commands translate worksheet data into a visual image of lines, bars, or segments of a circle. Unlike a list of numbers, **graphs** show pictorial *relationships* among numbers; this makes data analysis clearer and faster than with numbers alone. Many business presentations include graphs that communicate statistics in a simple, yet effective manner.

A graph usually depicts only some of the values on a worksheet. The series of rows and/or columns to be graphed is called the **data range**. Several graphs may be created for the same worksheet. The graphs may be the same type but use different data ranges, or they may be different types of graphs.

NOTE

The series of rows or columns used for a graph is called the data range.

Graphs can be viewed on screen or printed. If you have a color monitor, you can view graphs in color. You can print in color if you have a color printer.

The steps required to complete a graph are shown in Figure 13-1.

1.	Create the worksheet
2.	Create the graph.
3.	View and edit the graph.
4.	Name the graph.
5.	**In Release 2.x, save the graph on disk for printing.**
6.	Save the worksheet.
7.	Print the graph

Figure 13-1
The steps required to complete a graph.

TYPES OF GRAPHS

1-2-3 allows you to create several types of graphs, as you can see in Figure 13-2. The type of graph you select depends on the type of worksheet data and the purpose of the graph.

NOTE

The type of graph you select depends on the type of data in the worksheet and the purpose of the graph.

TYPE OF GRAPH	PURPOSE	RANGES TO USE
LINE	Plots change over time. Each line is a data range, each line point is a value in the range.	A-F: Up to 6 data ranges or lines. X: Labels identify points on lines.
BAR	Compares individual values or sets of values to one another. Each bar represents one value.	A: Range for single bar graph. A-F: Ranges for multiple bar graph. X: Labels identify the bars.
XY	Shows relationship between two types of numeric data. Each point is a value.	A-F: Up to 6 values in each cluster. X: Values shown on the X-axis.
STACK BAR	Compares individual and total values by stacking various bars on top of each other in a single bar.	A-F: A value from each range becomes part of a bar. X: Labels identify the bars.
PIE	Identifies the relationship of each value in a data range to the entire data range.	A: Values for pie slices. B: Patterns, colors, or exploding pie slices. X: Labels for individual pie slices.
HLCO	Tracks changes in high, low, closing, and opening prices of stocks or similar uses.	A-D: High, low, closing, opening ranges. X: Labels identify HLCO lines.
MIXED	Combine lines and bars in the same graph.	A-C: Ranges for bars. D-F: Ranges for lines. X: Labels identify bars and lines.

Figure 13-2
Types of graphs and how to use them.

ELEMENTS OF A GRAPH

Graphs are designed using the traditional concept of plotting points on X-Y axes. The vertical Y-axis and the horizontal X-axis, as well as graph options, are labeled in Figure 13-3. Refer to the figure as you construct your graphs in this section.

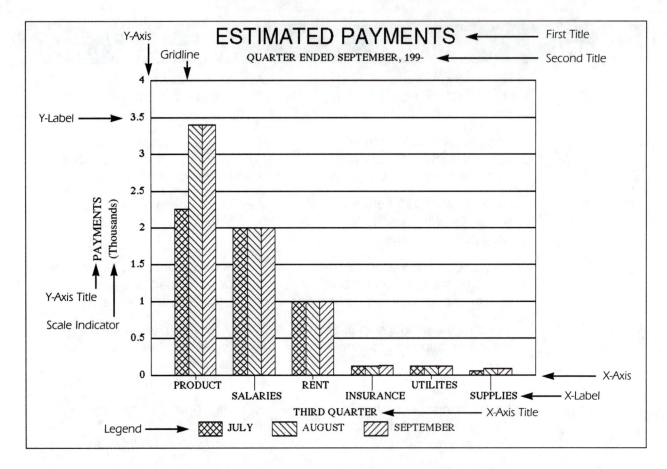

Figure 13-3
The elements of a graph.

Find the following graphic elements as you study Figure 13-3.

The **Y-axis** is a line along the left side of the graph with the vertical data points.

Y labels, set by 1-2-3 according to the data range, describe the data points on the Y-axis.

The **Y-axis title** describes the Y-axis.

The **Scale indicator** shows the units, such as thousands or millions, of the Y-axis.

The **X-axis** is a line at the bottom of a graph with horizontal data points.

X labels describe the data points on the X-axis.

The **X-axis title** describes the X-axis.

The **Legend** is a caption that identifies each data range.

A **First title** and a **Second title** identify the graph.

Grid lines are horizontal or vertical lines that begin at each data point.

QUICK QUESTIONS

1. What is the purpose of the 1-2-3 Graph commands?
2. Why do graphs make data analysis faster and easier?
3. What is a data range?
4. What is the first step in creating a graph?
5. How do you determine the type of graph to select?
6. What is the name for the vertical axis of a graph?
7. What is the name for the horizontal axis of a graph?
8. What is the purpose of the First and Second Titles of a graph?
9. Which graph element is automatically set by 1-2-3?
10. What is the purpose of the X labels?
11. What is a legend?

LINE GRAPHS

As you can see in Figure 13-4, **line graphs** are used to show change over time. Refer to this chart as you create line graphs; it will guide you in making graph selections.

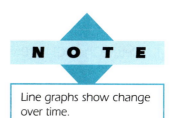

NOTE

Line graphs show change over time.

LINE GRAPH

Purpose: Plots changes in data over time. Each line depicts a data range, each point on the line represents a value in the data range.
A-F: up to 6 data ranges or lines (one data range per line)
X: X labels (identify the points on the lines)

Figure 13-4
Line graph information.

Part of the ACT101B worksheet is shown in Figure 13-5. Because the data shows change over a three-month period, a line graph would be an appropriate type of graph to use in this situation.

```
A15: [W15] '    SALARIES
         A            B           C           D           E
1    QUALITY OFFICE SUPPLIES
2    ESTIMATED RECEIPTS AND PAYMENTS
3    FOR THE QUARTER ENDED SEPTEMBER 199-
4    ==========================================================
5       DESCRIPTION      JULY       AUGUST    SEPTEMBER    TOTAL
6
7    RECEIPTS
8       SALES          $4,500.00   $6,800.00  $6,800.00  $18,100.00
9       SERVICE         6,200.00    8,500.00   8,000.00   22,700.00
10                     ------------------------------------------
11      TOTAL         $10,700.00  $15,300.00 $14,800.00  $40,800.00
12
```

Figure 13-5
Data ranges A and B.

The data to be graphed are the July, August, and September Sales and Service Receipts figures. Data range A will consist of the Sales amounts in cells B8, C8, and D8. Data range B will consist of the Service amounts in cells B9, C9, and D9. Each data range will produce one line of this two-line graph.

A legend will identify the Sales and Service lines. The points on each line will be the months, so the X labels will be July, August, and September. Figure 13-6 shows the completed graph.

1. Retrive the ACT101B worksheet.

GRAPH MENU. Activate the Graph menu.

2. Key /**G**raph.

TYPE. Set the type of graph (line, bar, pie, etc.).

3. Key **T**ype **L**ine.

DATA RANGES. Set the data ranges for each line, range A and range B.

4. Key (**A**) for data range A.

5. [B8] Key (**.**) to anchor the data range.

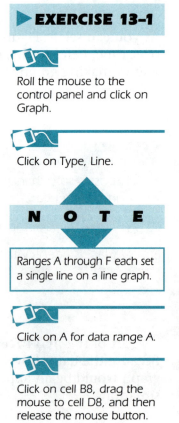

EXERCISE 13-1

Roll the mouse to the control panel and click on Graph.

Click on Type, Line.

N O T E

Ranges A through F each set a single line on a line graph.

Click on A for data range A.

Click on cell B8, drag the mouse to cell D8, and then release the mouse button.

6. [D8] Key **ENTER** to end the data range.

Click the left mouse button to end the data range.

7. Key **B** for data range B.

Click on B for data range B.

8. [B9] **.** to anchor the data range.

Click on cell B9, drag the mouse to cell D9, and then release the mouse button.

9. [D9] **ENTER** to end the data range.

Click the left mouse button to end the data range.

X LABELS. Set the X labels to identify the data points on the lines.

Each data point on a line is identified with an X label.

10. Key **X** for data range X.

Click on X for data range X.

11. Anchor B5 as the beginning of the range and D5 as the end of the range.

Click on cell B5, drag the mouse to cell D5, release the mouse button, and then click the left mouse button to set the X range at B5..D5.

12. Key **V**iew or **F10** to view the graph.

Click on View or press <F10> to view the graph.

LEGENDS. Now, create the legends. Two lines appear, with three data points at July, August, and September. However, the lines are not identified; both lines (ranges A and B) require a legend. The Y labels have been set by 1-2-3.

A legend is used to identify each line in a line graph.

13. Key **F10** to return to the Graph menu.

14. Key **O**ptions **L**egend **A**.

Click on Options, Legend, A.

15. Key **S**ales $\boxed{\text{ENTER}}$.

Key Sales and then click the left button.

16. Key **L**egend $\boxed{\text{B}}$.

Click on Legend, B.

17. Key **S**ervice $\boxed{\text{ENTER}}$.

Key Service and then click the left button.

18. Key **Q**uit to quit the Options menu.

Click on Quit to quit the Options menu.

19. Key $\boxed{\text{F10}}$ to view the graph.

FIRST AND SECOND TITLES. You now need to work on First and Second titles. The data range lines are identified, but the purpose or contents of the graph is not. Add a First and Second Title at the top of the graph.

Titles identify the purpose or contents of a graph.

20. Key $\boxed{\text{F10}}$ to return to the Graph menu.
21. Key **O**ptions **T**itles **F**irst.

Click on Options, Titles, First.

22. Key ESTIMATED RECEIPTS $\boxed{\text{ENTER}}$.
23. Key **T**itles **S**econd.

Click on Titles, Second.

24. Key Quarter Ended September 199- $\boxed{\text{ENTER}}$.
25. Key **Q**uit to quit the Options menu.

Click on Quit.

26. View the graph. Your completed graph should look like Figure 13-6.

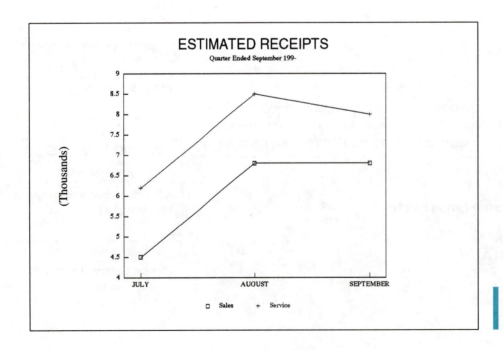

Figure 13-6
A line graph of the Estimated Receipts.

27. Analyze the graph to answer the following questions.
    a. Which brings more receipts, sales or service?
    b. Is the difference between sales and service receipts about the same for each month?
    c. What is the **amount** of the lowest monthly receipt?
    d. What is the **amount** of the highest monthly receipt?
    e. What is the smallest Y label?
    f. What is the increment (amount of change) of the Y labels?
28. Key **F10** to return to the Graph menu.

SAVE A GRAPH

If you are using 1-2-3 Release 2.x, you must use the **Graph Save** command to be able to print your graphs; this command is not necessary in Release 3.x. However, a graph stored on disk by itself through the Graph Save command can be used with other programs that accept graphics.

Give a graph a file name that suggests the worksheet it was created from and/or the type of graph, such as pie or bar. As with all DOS files, a file name can be up to *eight characters* in length; 1-2-3 will add a .PIC (Release 2.x) or .CGM (Release 3.x) extension. PIC and CGM files cannot be retrieved into a worksheet; only .WK1 or .WK3 files can be retrieved into a worksheet.

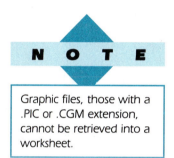

Graphic files, those with a .PIC or .CGM extension, cannot be retrieved into a worksheet.

NAME A GRAPH

When you enter new graph settings, previous settings are lost. To use several graphs within a worksheet, give each graph a name using the **Graph Name Create** command. Named graphs will remain with their worksheet and will retain their settings, and they can be viewed whenever the worksheet is active. A graph name can be up to *15 characters* in length. Once a graph is named, it can be made the current graph so you can view it with the command **Graph Name Use**.

Name graphs with the Graph Name Create command. View a named graph with the Graph Name Use command.

SAVE A WORKSHEET

Once a graph is given a name with the Name Create command, it may be used in the future only if the worksheet it was generated in is saved on disk. The worksheet is saved, as all worksheets have been, with the File Save command.

If you are using Release 2.x, save the graph on disk as a graphic file called PR13LINE. (1-2-3 will add a .PIC extension.) This will enable you to print the graphic later. Skip this step if you are using Release 3.x.

1. **Key Save PR13LINE ENTER** from the Graph menu in Release 2.x.

From the graph menu, choose the Name Create command to give the line graph you created the name PRAC13LINE. Then you can make the PRAC13LINE graph the current graph any time you retrieve the current worksheet.

2. **Key Name Create PRAC13LINE ENTER**.

3. **Key Quit** to quit the Graph menu.

After you name graphs, you must save the worksheet that contains them, or the graphs will be lost. As usual, the worksheet file name can be up to eight characters in length and will automatically be given a .WK1 or .WK3 extension.

4. **Key / File Save PRAC13A ENTER**.

▶ **EXERCISE 13–2**

Click on Save and then key PR13LINE. Click the left mouse button.

Click on Name, Create, and then key PRAC13LINE. Click the left mouse button.

Click on Quit to quit the Graph menu.

QUICK QUESTIONS

1. What is the purpose of line graphs?
2. What does each line represent on a line graph?
3. What does each point represent on a line graph?
4. What is the purpose of X labels?
5. What is the purpose of a legend for a line graph?
6. What do you add to a graph to identify the purpose of the graph?
7. What do you key to exit from the Options menu?
8. How can a graph saved on disk with the Graph Save command be used?
9. What is the purpose of naming graphs?
10. What command do you use to make a named graph the current graph?
11. Why is it necessary to save a worksheet when you have named its graphs?

BAR GRAPHS

Bar graphs, used to compare values to one another, can take the form of **single bar**, **multiple bar**, and **stack bar**. (A multiple bar graph is shown in Figure 13-3 on page 178.) Figure 13-7 shows the ranges for a bar graph.

BAR GRAPH
Compares individual values or sets of values to one another. Each bar represents one value (bar) or several values (stack bar).
A: the range of bars for a single bar graph
A-F: multiple ranges for a multiple bar graph (one data range per bar) or stack bar (a value from each range becomes part of a bar)
X: X labels identify the bars

Figure 13-7
Bar graph information.

SINGLE BAR GRAPHS

To learn more about single bar graphs, create one that compares the individual verbal scores of students on a college exam. Since you will use a file that is sorted on the verbal scores, the bars should be in descending heights. A completed single bar graph is shown in Figure 13-8.

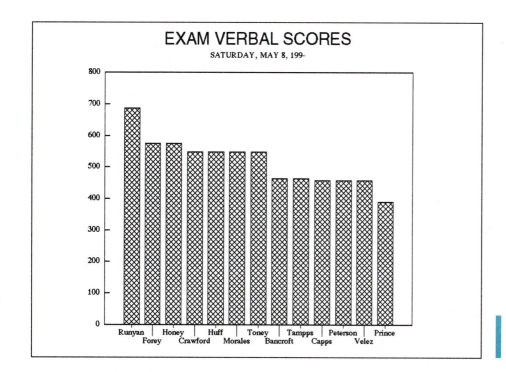

Figure 13-8
A single bar graph of the verbal exam scores.

LESSON 13 GRAPHS 185

From this point on, repetitive keyboard and mouse actions are not always explained in detail; many steps are left to the expertise of the student.

1. Retrieve the ACT111C worksheet.

Activate the Graph menu and select the type of graph.

2. Key / **G**raph **T**ype **B**ar.

DATA RANGE. Set the data range — use the verbal scores as Range A for the bars.

3. Key [A] for data range A.

4. [D7] Anchor the data range.

5. [D19] Key [ENTER] to end the data range.

View the graph.

6. Key [F10] to view the graph.

There are 13 students in the worksheet; you should see 13 bars. The values on the Y-axis (the verbal scores) are automatically displayed by 1-2-3 based on the values you set in the data range.

What is missing that would make the graph more meaningful? There are no labels describing what the bars are, and there are no titles identifying the graph.

7. Key [F10] to return to the Graph menu.

X LABELS. Add X labels to describe the bars.

8. Key [X] for data range X.

9. Set the label range from A7 to A19.

10. View the graph.

The names are too long for the distance between the bars; reading them is difficult. To remedy this, return to the worksheet and rekey shorter text (the last names only) in a blank area of the worksheet. (This extra step is necessary only in similar situations.)

11. Key [F10] to return to the Graph menu.

12. Key **Q**uit to return to the worksheet.

13. Go to G7 and key Runyan.

14. Key [↓] and then key the last name only for each student through G19. Check the accuracy of your keying.

Generate the Graph menu again so you can reset the X range. **The previous settings remain until you change them, reset them with the Graph Reset command, or make a new graph.** The graph Type and A range are correct. Reset the X-range of labels only.

15. Key / **G**raph.

EXERCISE 13-3

Click on Graph, Type, Bar.

Click on A for data range A.

Click on cell D7, drag the mouse to cell D19, and then release the mouse button.

Click the left mouse button to end the data range.

X labels describe the bars on a bar graph.

Click on X for data range X.

Previous graph settings remain until they are changed or reset, or until a new graph is made.

16. Key [X] and then press [ESC] to cancel the old range. (Or press the right mouse button to cancel the old range.)

17. Set the range from G7 to G19.

18. View the graph.

The graph is clearer now, but there is no indication that these are verbal scores or when the exam was taken. Add titles to the graph.

19. Key [ESC] to return to the Graph menu.

FIRST TITLE. Add the First title.

20. Key **O**ptions **T**itles **F**irst.

The first title is the most important one.

21. Key EXAM VERBAL SCORES [ENTER].

SECOND TITLE. Add the Second title.

22. Key **T**itles **S**econd.

23. Key SATURDAY, MAY 8, 199- [ENTER].

24. Key **Q**uit to quit the Options menu.

25. View the graph.

The graph is complete and should look like Figure 13-8. **Save the graph as a graphic file if you are using Release 2.x.** Name the graph and save the worksheet before continuing.

26. Key [F10] to exit View.

If you are using Release 2.x save the graph as a .PIC file.

27. **Key Save PR13SBAR [ENTER].**

Name the graph.

28. Key **N**ame **C**reate PRAC13SBAR [ENTER].

29. Key **Q**uit to return to the worksheet screen.

Save the worksheet.

30. Key / **F**ile **S**ave PRAC13B.

31. Keep the worksheet on your screen for the next exercise.

MULTIPLE BAR GRAPH

Multiple bar graphs compare sets of values to one another. You will construct a graph that compares the verbal scores with math scores for individual students. The verbal scores will be one data range, and the math scores will be a second data range.

N O T E

Multiple bar graphs compare sets of values to each other.

> **EXERCISE 13-4**

1. Refer to Figure 13-7 on page 185 to see the settings available for a multiple bar graph.

As you recall, previous settings remain in effect until you change them. The type is still bar, and the A range is already set for the verbal scores. Set the next range, B, for the math scores.

2. Activate the Graph menu.
3. Key **B** for the B range.
4. Set the B range from E7 to E19.
5. View the graph.

The graph shows a double bar for each person. One bar is the verbal score. The other bar is the math score. But which is which? Create a legend that will show which bar represents verbal scores and which bar represents math scores.

6. Key **F10** to exit from View.

Key the legend.

7. Key **O**ptions **L**egend.

Range A is verbal and range B is math.

8. Key **A** for range A.
9. Key Verbal **ENTER**.
10. Key **L**egend **B**.
11. Key Math **ENTER**.
12. Key **T**itles **F**irst to change the First Title to reflect the new data.
13. Key the title EXAM VERBAL & MATH SCORES **ENTER**.
14. Key **Q**uit to end the Options menu.
15. View the graph.

Data is displayed clearly and completely. Check your graph against Figure 13-9. Save the graph (Release 2.x), name the graph, and save the worksheet.

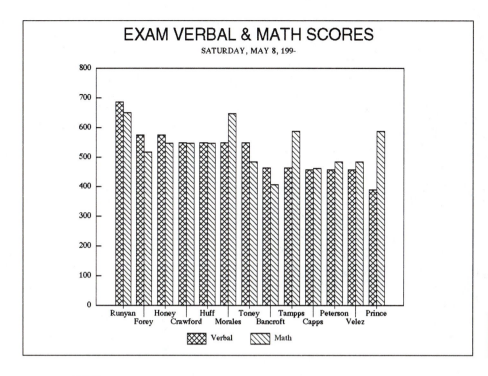

Figure 13-9
A multiple bar graph for verbal and math scores.

16. Key **F10** to exit from View.

If you are using Release 2.x, save the graph as a .PIC file.

17. **In Release 2.x, key Save PR13MBAR ENTER.**

Name the graph and then save the worksheet.

18. Key **N**ame **C**reate PRAC13MBAR **ENTER**.

19. Key **Q**uit to exit the Graph menu.

Save the worksheet so the named graphic will be stored with it.

20. Key / **F**ile **S**ave PRAC13B **ENTER**. Key **R**eplace.

STACK BAR GRAPH

Stack bar graphs compare individual and total values by stacking various bars on top of each other in a single bar. A value from each range becomes part of a bar.

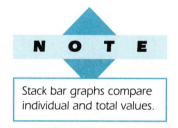

Stack bar graphs compare individual and total values.

1. Use the PRAC13B worksheet to create a stack bar graph.

The settings from the last graph (the multiple bar graph) are still in effect. Simply tell 1-2-3 to create a stack bar graph using those settings.

2. Key / **G**raph **T**ype **S**tack-Bar.

View the completed graph, shown in Figure 13-10. Each bar displays the total score for a student, a combination of verbal and math scores.

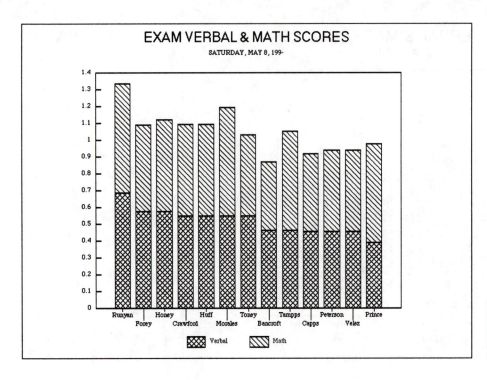

Figure 13-10
The verbal and math scores in the form of a stack bar graph.

3. Return to the Grap**h** menu.

If you are using Release 2.x, save the graph as a .PIC file.

4. **In Release 2.x Key Save PR13TBAR** ENTER.

Name the graph and then save the worksheet.

5. Key **N**ame **C**reate PRAC13TBAR ENTER.
6. Key **Q**uit to exit the Graph menu.
7. Key / **F**ile **S**ave PRAC13B. Key **R**eplace.

QUICK QUESTIONS

1. What is the purpose of bar graphs?
2. How many data ranges will you have in a single bar graph?
3. How does 1-2-3 determine the values on the Y-axis?
4. What can you do if X labels are too long to be readable?
5. What three actions will change a previous graph setting?
6. What is the name of the second range in a multiple bar graph?
7. How is a stack bar graph different from an ordinary bar graph?

PIE GRAPHS

Pie graphs, used to show portions of a whole, involve only one data range. Figure 13-11 shows some of the settings for pie graphs.

PIE GRAPH
Identifies the relationship of each value in a data range to the entire data range.
A: the values in one data range that you want to show as pie slices
B: values that control hatch patterns, colors, or explosion of pie slices
X: the labels for the individual pie slices

> **NOTE**
>
> Pie graphs show portions of a whole.

Figure 13-11
Pie graph information.

You can enhance a pie graph by shading the pieces and/or **exploding** (separating) one or more important pieces. Range B, which controls shading and exploding, must be keyed into a blank area of the worksheet. The number of cells used for range B must equal the number of slices in the pie.

In Release 2.x, the shading values to key in range B vary from 1 to 8. In Release 3.x, the shading values in range B vary from 1 to 14. If you are using a color monitor, the shading values will display the pie pieces in various colors. If you have a monochrome monitor, the shading values will display various hatch patterns. Add 100 to the shading values of cells to explode pieces of pie.

> **NOTE**
>
> In a pie chart, range B controls the shading and/or explosion of pie pieces.

> **NOTE**
>
> In Release 2.x, the shading values may range from 1 to 8. In Release 3.x, the shading values may range from 1 to 14.

GRAPH RESET

Graph settings may be cleared with the **Graph Reset** command. After you choose Reset, you may choose Graph to clear all graph settings; X, A, B, C, D, E, F to clear individual ranges; Ranges to clear all ranges; or Options to clear all options.

You will create a pie graph that shows the relationship of individual cell values in an @SUM range to the total value. The completed graph is shown in Figure 13-12.

▶ **EXERCISE 13-6**

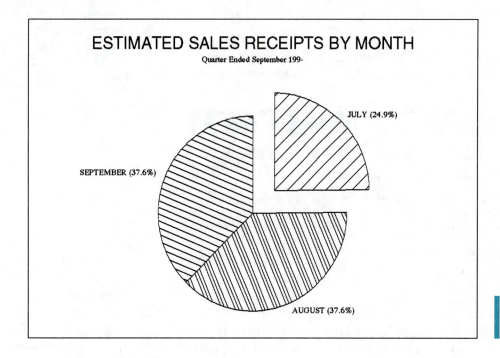

Figure 13-12
A pie graph with the July piece exploded.

1. Retrieve the PRAC13A worksheet.

First, reset all options from the last graph created in this worksheet using the Graph Reset Graph command.

2. Key / **G**raph **R**eset **G**raph.

The Graph Reset command resets options from the previous graph.

To show the Sales Receipts for each month in relation to the total for the quarter, use Estimated Sales Receipts at B8 to D8 for the data range. Use the months at B5 to D5 as the X labels for the pie slices.

3. Key **T**ype **P**ie.
4. Key **A** to set the data range for the slices of pie.
5. Set data range A from B8 through D8.
6. Key **X** to set the labels for the slices of pie.
7. Set the X label range from B5 to D5.
8. View the graph. It is informative, but it needs graph identification titles.
9. Key **F10** to exit the view.
10. Key **O**ption **T**itles **F**irst.
11. Key ESTIMATED SALES RECEIPTS BY MONTH **ENTER**.
12. Key **T**itles **S**econd.
13. Key Quarter Ended September 199- **ENTER**.
14. Key **Q**uit to exit the Option menu.
15. View the graph and then press **F10** **Q**uit to return to the worksheet.

PIE SHADING. In a blank area of the worksheet, key values that will shade the pie pieces and explode the first piece of pie. For three pieces of pie, you will need three shading values, each displaying a unique color or hatch pattern. The values can be from 1 to 8 (Release 2.x) or 1 to 14 (Release 3.x). Key the values 7, 4, and 2, but add 100 to the first value to explode that piece. (100 + 7 = 107.) The three values will be used as Range B (A30..C30), corresponding to the three pie pieces in Range A (B8..D8). (The values will appear as decimals due to global format.)

N O T E

In a blank area of the worksheet, key a value for every cell in range A. Add 100 to a value to explode a piece of pie.

16. [A30] 107 → (A shading value and explosion for cell B8; a shading value of 7 + 100 to explode)

17. [B30] 4 → (a shading value for cell C8)

18. [C30] 2 **ENTER** (a shading value for cell D8)

Set the B range in the Graph menu.

19. Key / **G**raph **B** for range B.

20. Anchor A30 as the beginning of the range and C30 as the end of the range.

21. View your graph. It should look like Figure 13-12. Exit the view.

Name your graph.

22. Key **N**ame **C**reate PRAC13PIE **ENTER**.

23. **If you are using Release 2.2, use the Graph Save command to save the graph as a .PIC file called PR13PIE.**

24. Exit the Graph menu.

25. Save the worksheet as PRAC13C.

PRINT GRAPHS

The method of printing graphs varies with the 1-2-3 release you are using. If you are using Release 3.x, use the directions for Exercise 13-7, *RELEASE 3.X PRINTING*. If you are using Release 2.x, begin with the directions for Exercise 13-8, *RELEASE 2.X PRINTING*.

(Release 3.x Printing)

Use **Print Image Current** to print the current graph or **Print Image Named-Graph** to print a graph you have named.

To print the line graph you named PRAC13LINE that is a part of the PRAC13C worksheet, follow the steps below.

1. Retrieve the PRAC13C worksheet.

2. Key / **P**rint **I**mage **N**amed-Graph PRAC13LINE **ENTER** **A**lign **G**o.

Be patient; it may take a few minutes for your printer to begin printing the graph.

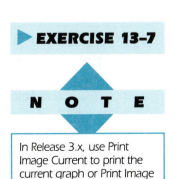

▶ **EXERCISE 13-7**

N O T E

In Release 3.x, use Print Image Current to print the current graph or Print Image Named-Graph to print a graph you have named.

3. When printing is complete, press **q** to quit the Print menu.
4. Print the remaining named graph in this worksheet, PRAC13PIE.
5. Retrieve the PRAC13B worksheet. Print the named graphs PRAC13SBAR, PRAC13MBAR, and PRAC13TBAR.

(Release 2.x Printing)

▶ **EXERCISE 13-8**

To print graphs, you must exit from 1-2-3 and enter the Lotus PrintGraph program. The graphs are stored in the .PIC graphic files that you saved.

1. Key **/ Q**uit **Y**es (**Y**es if asked to verify) to exit from 1-2-3.

Next, you will enter the PrintGraph program, a separate utility program that comes with the Lotus 1-2-3 software. PrintGraph can only print .PIC files.

2. To enter PrintGraph, quit Lotus and then load Print Graph:

If you return to the Lotus Access Menu; key **P**rintGraph.

If you return to the system prompt, either remain in the Lotus 1-2-3 directory or change to the Lotus 1-2-3 directory. You must be in the Lotus directory to enter PrintGraph. Key pgraph **ENTER** to enter PrintGraph.

If you return to the Dosshell, exit the Dosshell and change to the Lotus 1-2-3 directory. Key pgraph **ENTER** to enter PrintGraph.

The PrintGraph screen looks similar to Figure 13-13.

```
Select graphs to print or preview
Image-Select  Settings  Go  Align  Page  Exit

    GRAPHS    IMAGE SETTINGS                      HARDWARE SETTINGS
   TO PRINT   Size                Range colors    Graphs directory
              Top        .395     X                 C:\123R23
              Left       .750     A               Fonts directory
              Width     6.500     B                 C:\123R23
              Height    4.691     C               Interface
              Rotation   .000     D                 Parallel 1
                                  E               Printer
              Font                F
              1  BLOCK1                           Paper size
              2  BLOCK1                             Width    8.500
                                                   Length  11.000
```

Figure 13-13
The PrintGraph screen.

3. Check the Hardware Settings for the current **Graphs directory**. This is where you have been saving all the files you create. If the settings are incorrect, select **S**ettings **H**ardware **G**raphs-Directory and then enter the path of your .PIC files.

4. Check all settings for accuracy, particularly your printer selection. The printer can be reset with **S**ettings **H**ardware **P**rinter.

5. Key **Q**uit **Q**uit when you are done with the Graphic directory.

6. Key **S**ettings **A**ction **E**ject **Y**es **Q**uit **Q**uit to advance paper to the top after printing each graph.

7. Key **I**mage-**S**elect to view the names of all .PIC files.

You may check the files you wish to print below:

Graph Name

____ PR13LINE

____ PR13SBAR

____ PR13MBAR

____ PR13TBAR

____ PR13PIE

8. From the Image-Select screen, press **ENTER** on a single file you want to print or press **SPACE BAR** to mark or unmark a group of files for printing. Press **ENTER** when all files are marked.

9. Key **A**lign **G**o at the main PrintGraph menu.

10. Key **E**xit **Y**es when you have completed printing.

QUICK QUESTIONS

1. What is the purpose of pie graphs?
2. How many data ranges can you use for a pie graph?
3. What command will cancel all previous graph settings?
4. What data range is used for the shading values for a pie graph?
5. (Release 3.x users) What command do you use to print graphs?
6. (Release 2.x users) What option should you choose from the PrintGraph main menu to see a list of your .PIC files for printing?

NEW COMMANDS AND KEYS

/ Graph. Activates the Graph menu.

/ Graph Type. Sets the type of graph, such as line, bar, or pie.

F10. Displays the current graph or returns to the Graph menu from the view.

/ Graph X. Establishes the range for the X labels.

/ Graph A-F. Establishes the range for a line, bar, or pie graph.

/ Graph Options Legend. Creates legends for data ranges.

/ Graph Options Titles. Displays up to two identifying lines of text at the top of a graph.

/ Graph Name Create. Gives a name to a worksheet graph so it can be reused in the future.

/ Graph Name Use. Retrieves a named graph, making it the current graph.

/ Graph Save. Saves the current graph in a file for printing or use in other programs.

/ Graph Reset. Resets some or all graph settings.

/ Print Image Current. Prints the current graph in Release 3.x.

/ Print Image Named-Graph. Prints a named graph.

FILES CREATED IN THIS LESSON

PRAC13A
PRAC13B
PRAC13C
ACT131
ACT132
ACT133
CTP13

NAMED GRAPHS IN THIS LESSON

PRAC13LINE
PRAC13SBAR
PRAC13MBAR
PRAC13TBAR
PRAC13PIE
ACT131SBAR
ACT131MBAR
ACT131TBAR
ACT132PIE
ACT133LINE
CTP113A
CTP13B
CTP13C
CTP13D

SAVED GRAPHS IN THIS LESSON

PR13LINE
PR13SBAR
PR13MBAR
PR13TBAR
PR13PIE
AC131SBR
AC131MBR
AC131TBR
AC132PIE
ACT133LN
CTP13A
CTP13B
CTP13C
CTP13D

ACTIVITIES

ACTIVITY 13-1

Generate a single bar graph, a multiple bar graph, and a stack bar graph.

1. Retrieve the PRAC13A worksheet. Use the Reset command to clear the previous graph settings.

2. Create a single bar graph to compare the amounts of the July estimated payments in cells B14 to B19. This is Range A.

3. Range X, the X-axis labels that identify the bars, are the labels in cells A14 to A19.

4. The First Title is: ESTIMATED PAYMENTS. The Second Title is: July, 199-.

5. View the graph and make any necessary corrections. Name the graph ACT131SBAR. *If you have Release 2.x, save the graph as AC131SBR.*

6. Create a multiple bar graph to compare the amounts of the July, August, and September estimated payments. Range A remains from the single bar graph. Range B is the August values, cells C14 to C19. Range C is the September values, cells D14 to D19. Range X, the labels, remains.

7. Add appropriate First and Second Titles at the top.

8. Add a Legend for each bar. Legend A is July, B is August, and C is September.

9. View the graph. Name it ACT131MBAR. *If you have Release 2.x, save the graph as AC131MBR.*

10. Change the type of the current graph to stack bar. Name it ACT131TBAR. *If you are using Release 2.2, save the graph as AC131TBR.*

11. Save the worksheet as ACT131. Print the three graphs following the printing directions for your release of 1-2-3.

Create a pie graph using the PRAC13A worksheet.

ACTIVITY 13-2

1. Use the Graph Reset command to clear the previous graph.
2. Display the relationship of the three-month total of the Product, Salaries, and Rent Payments, cells E14 to E16. This is the A Range.
3. Range X, the pie-slice labels, are the names of the Payment items. These are in cells A14 to A16.
4. Use the First Title TOTAL ESTIMATED PAYMENTS. The Second Title is: Quarter Ended September 1993.
5. Quit the Graph menu. In a blank area of the worksheet, key range B to shade the pie pieces. Since there are three pie pieces, range B should contain three cells. Explode the smallest pie piece.
6. Name the graph as ACT132PIE. *If you have Release 2.x, save the graph as AC132PIE.* Save the worksheet as ACT132.
7. Print the pie graph.

ACTIVITY 13-3

Create a line graph using the PRAC13A worksheet.

1. Use the / Graph Reset command to clear the previous graph.
2. The graph will have two lines. Range A will show changes in the estimated total Receipts for the period of July, August, and September (B11.D11). Range B will show changes in the estimated total Payments for the three months (B21.D21).
3. The points on the line, the X-axis labels, are the months of July, August, and September.
4. Key appropriate First and Second Titles. Key Legends for each line.
5. Name the graph ACT133LINE. *If you are using Release 2.x, save the graph as ACT133LN.* Save the worksheet as ACT133. Print the line graph.

CRITICAL THINKING PROJECT 13

Choose a worksheet from your disk to create four types of meaningful graphs; choose types that suit the data. Each one should contain graph options that promote understanding of the graph. Name the graphs CTP13A, CTP13B, CTP13C, and CTP13D, save the graphs if necessary as CTP13A, CTP13B, CTP13C and CTP13D, and save the worksheet as CTP13. Print the graphs.

Attach an analysis of the information displayed by each graph; use a word processor for this, or make column A a width of 72 and key each analysis in a blank worksheet. If helpful, you can reference the analysis you did in Exercise 13-1, step 27.

Turn in each graph with its attached analysis.

LESSON 14

Advanced Application — Balloon Biz

OBJECTIVES

- Apply spreadsheet knowledge to new situations
- Reconstruct spreadsheets using a variety of skills, including label and number format and column width
- Determine appropriate formulas and functions and copy them
- Edit worksheets by inserting, deleting, and moving rows and columns
- View, manipulate, and print wide worksheets
- Print with page breaks, borders, and headers
- Sort, find, and extract data
- Construct and print graphs

Estimated Time: 5 hours (3-1/2 hours with template files)

YOUR NEW POSITION

You have been hired to work part time at Balloon Biz, a store that specializes in balloon arrangements. Jill Long, the owner of Balloon Biz, selected you over several other applicants for the job because of your Lotus 1-2-3 computer skills.

Jill keeps all of her business records on the computer, and she is having you assume responsibility for the following computer tasks:

- maintain a general journal.
- keep inventory records.
- maintain customer and vendor databases.
- prepare special financial statements.

CUSTOMER DATABASE

Customer billing is made from the Customer database, shown in Figure SBA1. Update it each day from sales on account entries in the general journal. Increase Amt Owed when a customer makes a purchase on account; decrease Amt Owed and increase Amt Paid when a payment is received from a customer.

BALLOON BIZ
CUSTOMER DATABASE

SS#	NAME	COMPANY	ADDRESS	ZIP	AMT OWED	AMT PAID	DATE PAID	BALANCE
525-60-8284	Elaine Dobbins	Eastview High	4838 E 82	94417	15.5	0		
614-32-3381	Byron Klemann	Beachway Hospital	3782 N Denny	94463	38.72	12.85	03/01/–	
884-38-6972	Hattie Powell	Parties To Go	2605 Brandonway	94436	78.42	37.5	02/05/–	
405-66-3742	Isako Eto	Third Bank	1156 Victory Dr	94472	0	0	01/30/–	
339-57-9093	Sean Tuttle		7423 Marsh Rd	94404	27.26	0	01/28/–	
517-63-4412	E. L. Ensey	Ensey Catering	250 E Ohio	94460	63	56.64	02/17/–	
344-81-5407	Gloria Ramirez		14507 Towne Rd	94481	22.6	24.74	01/23/–	

Figure SBA1
Customer database.

▶ **EXERCISE 14-1**

1. Create the Customer database shown in Figure SBA1. (Or use Template File CUSTOMTP.) Format the labels and numbers as shown in Figure SBA1.

2. Edit the dates in the Date Paid column so they have the current year. Center the dates.

3. Calculate the Balance amounts in column I.

4. Leave a blank row below the worksheet and then total the three numeric columns in row 14. Key the label TOTAL at cell E14 to identify the column totals.

5. Save the worksheet as CUSTOM. Print it and keep it for reference.

VENDOR DATABASE

The Vendor database (Figure SBA2) is kept primarily for ordering merchandise and as a price reference. Update this database when notified of the following changes: a company goes out of business or we drop them as a vendor; there is a change in phone number or address; a contact person is replaced; an item is no longer available; or the cost of an item changes.

```
BALLOON BIZ
VENDOR DATABASE
-------------------------------------------------------------------------------
```

VEND #	COMPANY	PHONE	CONTACT	ADDRESS	CITY/ST	ZIP	ITEM #	COST	UNIT
136	The Party Store	703-227-8652	Gene Pate	911 W Village Dr	Reston, VA	22091	B3451C	1.38	EA
							B7892F	9	EA
							B3304B	10	EA
							46231MA	39	DOZ
108	Novelty Wholesale	508-225-7312	Sal Nelson	1141 Tulip St	Easthaven, MA	25681	TB0010	6.25	EA
							W373610	4.8	1 DOZ
114	Will Brothers	605-352-1716	Larry Will	1392 E New York	Sioux City SD	57049	7786-31	4.5	EA
							ARCH12	8.45	EA
							ARCH08	5.95	EA
189	Balloons Unlimited	800-469-9904	Cassie Stokes	2405 N Tremont	Jaffrey, NH	34527	7851FA	18	2 DOZ
							B4917M	38.5	100
156	Balloonmania	800-BAL-LOON	Katy Shore	8103 Wakefield	Terre Haute, IN	47809	B3451C	1.38	EA
							B7829F	9	EA
							B3304B	10	EA
262	Confection Ltd	412-571-7727	Dean Knop	6594 Palmer St	Bridgeville, PA	15017	C1-7782	3.75	EA
							C2-6723	6.25	EA

Figure SBA2
Vendor database.

EXERCISE 14-2

1. Create the Vendor database shown in Figure SBA2. (Or use Template File VENDORTP.) Improve the appearance of the numbers in the Cost column by formatting them so decimal points are aligned.
2. Save the database as VENDOR. Print it and keep it for reference.

INVENTORY RECORD

Changes in inventory are recorded daily. Increase an inventory item when a shipment arrives, and decrease an inventory item when a sale is made. Always check (using Data Query Extract) for any inventory item that has reached or is below the reorder point. If you find any such items, notify Jill in writing. Figure SBA3 shows the Inventory Record.

```
BALLOON BIZ
INVENTORY RECORD
------------------------------------------------------------------------
```

STOCK #	ITEM	ON HAND	REORDER PT	REORDER AMT	COST	UNIT	INVESTMT	VEND #
B3451C	Balloon w Confetti	30	21	12	1.38	EA		156
B7829F	Balloon w Flowers	5	3	10	9	EA		156
B3304B	Balloon w Bear	12	8	12	10	EA		156
7851FA	Balloons, Foil	22	16	12	18	2 DOZ		189
B4917M	Balloons, Mylar Plain	700	500	500	38.5	100		189
TB0010	Teddy Bear, Stuffed	5	3	5	6.25	EA		108
7786-31	Dog, Stuffed	3	2	3	4.5	EA		114
C1-7782	Chocolates, 1 lb Asstd	9	8	7	3.75	EA		262
C2-6723	Chocolates, 2 lb Asstd	7	5	5	6.25	EA		262
46231MA	Mug	14	8	12	39	1 DOZ		136
ARCH12	Arch Form Lrg	7	5	5	8.45	EA		114
ARCH08	Arch Form Med	9	5	5	5.95	EA		114
W373610	Weights, Asstd 10 oz	52	36	24	4.8	DOZ		108

Figure SBA3
Inventory Record.

▶ **EXERCISE 14–3**

1. Create the Inventory Record shown in Figure SBA3. (Or use Template File INVENTTP.)

2. Calculate the Investmt amounts by multiplying the number of items on hand times the cost.

3. Go to the Investmt column in each record where the Units is **not** EA. Use F2 to edit the Investmt amount so that it is divided by the Unit amount. For example, the Investmt amount for Stock# 7851FA (cell H9) is C9*F9/24. (Two dozen = 24.) You have four records to change in this way.

4. Leave a blank row below the worksheet and then total the Investmt column. Key the label TOTAL to identify the column total.

5. Improve the appearance of the numbers in the Cost and Investmt columns by formatting them so that decimals align.

6. Save the worksheet as INVENT. Print it and keep it for reference.

GENERAL JOURNAL

All daily transactions are recorded in the general journal, shown in Figure SBA4. Space is allowed for the balance brought forward from the previous week, and column headings show the categories you will consider for the transactions.

```
BALLOON BIZ
GENERAL JOURNAL
================================================================================
WEEK OF
Balance brought forward
--------------------------------------------------------------------------------
DATE   CHK NO   TRANSACTION   SALES   CASH   ACC REC   PURCH   ACC PAY   SAL   RENT   UTIL   MISC
```

Figure SBA4
General Journal.

As you create a journal entry for each transaction, be sure to include the following:

- the date.
- the check number if Balloon Biz wrote a check.
- a brief description of the transaction (indent second or third description lines).
- the dollar amount of the entry, recorded in *two* columns.

If the transaction *increases* an account, simply key the amount. If the transaction *decreases* an account, precede the amount with a *minus sign* (-). For example, when we make a sale, increase Sales and increase either Cash or Accounts Receivable.

EXPLANATION OF ACCOUNTS

The following information briefly describes the general journal accounts.

Sales This increases when a customer makes a purchase.

Cash This increases when we receive cash; it decreases when we pay cash.

Acc Rec (Accounts Receivable) This increases when a customer (from the Customer database) makes a purchase on account (promises to pay); this decreases when a customer makes a payment on their account.

Purch (Purchases) This increases when we receive goods from our vendors that we can sell.

Acc Pay (Accounts Payable) This increases when we receive goods from our vendor that we do not pay now; this decreases when we make a payment to our vendors.

Sal (Salaries) This increases when an employee is paid. This includes the owner's pay.

Rent This increases when we make a rent payment.

Util (Utilities) This increases when we make a payment on the electric, water, or phone bill.

Misc (Miscellaneous) This increases when we pay for something, such as advertising or a delivery expense, that is not covered in the listed accounts. It is important that the transaction description in the general journal fully explain miscellaneous expenses.

After you complete the general journal entries each day, update the Customer, Vendor, and Inventory files with increases and decreases according to the transactions.

▶ **EXERCISE 14-4**

1. Create the general journal shown in Figure SBA4. (Or use Template File JOURNTP.) Align all column headings at the right except Date and Transaction. Center the heading Date; left align the heading Transaction. Use a global fixed format with 2 decimal places.

2. Save the journal on disk as a template file (a file that is an empty form that can be retrieved and filled in when needed). Call the template file JOURTEMP.

3. Begin filling in the journal template for this week. This is the week of March 15-21, 19—. With the JOURTEMP file on your screen, key in cell F5 the Acc Rec Balance brought forward. Obtain this from the Total Balance in the CUSTOM file; refer to your printout of the CUSTOM file for the total of column I.

4. Record the Purch Balance brought forward in cell G5, obtained from the Total Investment in the INVENT file. Refer to your printout of the INVENT file.

5. Key the remaining Balances brought forward at the appropriate columns in row 5:

Sales	17,250.87
Cash	2,582.38
Accts Payable	276.18
Salaries (Sal)	4,080.00
Rent	2,000.00
Utilities	240.00
Miscellaneous	652.60

6. Save the worksheet for the current week and year with the name JR0315—. (Substitute the current year for the hyphens.)

DAILY PROCEDURE

When Jill leaves the store at 5 p.m., she will leave you notes of the daily transactions. Record the transactions in the general journal and then in other appropriate worksheets. Print them for Jill's return to work the following day.

The Balloon Biz Price List is used to determine sales amounts. You may do scratch calculations in an empty area of the worksheet and then erase them with the Range Erase command. Use the Titles and Window commands for large worksheets. Always use the current year in dates.

**BALLOON BIZ
PRICE LIST**

FOIL BALLOONS (EA.)	2.50
MYLAR BALLOONS (EA.)	1.35
CONFETTI IN BALLOON	4.25
FLOWERS IN BALLOON	18.00
BEAR IN BALLOON	20.00
STUFFED ANIMALS	6.50↑
CHOCOLATES	7.50↑
COFFEE MUGS	6.50
WEIGHTS (10 OZ.)	1.00
BALLOON ARCHES	INQUIRE
CENTERPIECES	INQUIRE
LOCAL DELIVERY FEE	5.00

DAY ONE - Monday, March 15.

▶ **EXERCISE 14-5**

Use the JR0315— worksheet to enter the following transactions for the day in the general journal. For a sales transaction, just write the type of transaction; it is not necessary to include a list of all the items purchased.

1. Sold balloon bouquet (charge card)

    1 confetti

    7 mylar

    Record the date **03/15/—** at cell A8. Key a brief description of the transaction at cell C8: **Sold 1 bouquet - charge**. Use the Price List to figure the selling price of each type of balloon. Use an empty part of the journal to calculate the total sale (4.25+7*1.35); record this as an increase in both the Sales and Cash columns. (A charge card sale is considered cash in the journal.) When done with the temporary calculations, erase them. Your journal entry should be similar to Figure SBA5.

```
BALLOON BIZ
GENERAL JOURNAL
================================================================================
WEEK OF March 15-21, 19-
Balance brought forward      17,250.87  2,582.38  113.77  780.15  276.18  4,080.00  2,000.00  240.00  652.60
--------------------------------------------------------------------------------
DATE      CHK NO  TRANSACTION           SALES    CASH    ACC REC  PURCH  ACC PAY    SAL      RENT    UTIL   MISC
03/15/-           Sold 1 bouquet - charge  13.70   13.70
```

Figure SBA5
Journal entry.

2. Sold balloon bouquet (cash)

   Bear in balloon

   4 mylar

   1 lb. chocolates

   Key the new transaction in row 9. It is not necessary to key the date again until it changes (on 03/16). You must look at your printed copy of the Inventory Record to determine the price of an item not on the price list. Items sell for 200% of cost. To find the sales price of the 1 lb. chocolates, find the cost in the Inventory Record. The cost is $3.75. 200% of $3.75 is 7.50. (3.75 * 2 = 7.50.)

3. Sold 10 balloon bouquets on account to Parties To Go.

   10 x 4 mylar

   10 x 1 foil

   10 x 1 weights

   <u>Deliver</u>

   <u>Each</u> bouquet had 4 mylar, 1 foil, and 1 weight. For sales on account, always include the customer's name in the journal entry. Calculate the sales price of all items, and do not forget to add the delivery fee. Sales on account increases Acc Rec, not Cash. Compare your journal with Figure SBA6. Figure SBA6 also shows part of the worksheet below the journal used for temporary calculations.

```
BALLOON BIZ
GENERAL JOURNAL
==============================================================================================
WEEK OF March 15-21, 19--
Balance brought forward            17,250.87  2,582.38  113.77  780.15  276.18  4,080.00  2,000.00  240.00  652.60
----------------------------------------------------------------------------------------------
DATE    CHK NO  TRANSACTION        SALES      CASH      ACC REC PURCH   ACC PAY SAL       RENT      UTIL    MISC
03/15/-         Sold 1 bouquet - charge   13.70   13.70
                Sold 1 bouquet - cash     32.90   32.90
                Sold 10 bouquets on acct  94.00           94.00
                  Parties To Go

                                           5.40
                                           2.50
                                           1.00
                                          89.00
                                          94.00
```

Figure SBA6
Journal check no. 1

4. Received check from Elaine Dobbins for $15.50 payment on account.

   Include the customer's name in the journal entry. Increase Cash but decrease Acc Rec by keying -15.50.

5. Subtotal all accounts that have amounts entered. Globally format for fixed, two decimal places. Check your work against Figure SBA7.

```
BALLOON BIZ
GENERAL JOURNAL
==============================================================================================
WEEK OF March 15-21, 19--
Balance brought forward            17,250.87  2,582.38  113.77  780.15  276.18  4,080.00  2,000.00  240.00  652.60
----------------------------------------------------------------------------------------------
DATE    CHK NO  TRANSACTION        SALES      CASH      ACC REC PURCH   ACC PAY SAL       RENT      UTIL    MISC
03/15/-         Sold 1 bouquet - charge   13.70   13.70
                Sold 1 bouquet - cash     32.90   32.90
                Sold 10 bouquets on acct  94.00           94.00
                  Parties To Go
                Received payment on account        15.50  -15.50
                  Elaine Dobbins
                SUBTOTALS                 140.60   62.10   78.50
```

Figure SBA7
Journal check no. 2

6. Print the journal worksheet and then save it on disk as JDAY1.

7. Use the copy of the journal you printed in step 6 to update the CUSTOM file with all transactions that affected the CUSTOM file. Remember, Acc Rec increases the Amt Owed column or the Amt Paid column of the CUSTOM file. To increase the Amt Owed for Parties To Go, at cell F8 press F2 to edit the current number and then key **+94.Enter**. To update

the Amt Paid column for Elaine Dobbins, enter the amount paid (15.50) in cell G6. Key the date at cell H6. Save the updated Customer file as CUSTOM1 and print it.

8. Use the Day One transaction descriptions to update the INVENT file. Items sold decrease the On Hand column and shipments increase the On Hand column. Always edit with the F2 key the cells to decrease in the On Hand column; this keeps a record of how each amount was decreased. For example, at C6 decrease the number of Confetti balloons by one by pressing F2 and then keying -1 **Enter**. Use an empty part of the worksheet for calculations.

9. Query the database to extract any items that have an On Hand amount equal to or below the Reorder Pt. The query criteria is On Hand <= Reorder Pt. To key this criteria, copy the field name ON HAND to cell A22; at cell A23, key +C6<=D6. The output range, beginning at A24, should include the Stock #, the Item description, the On Hand, and the Reorder Pt fields. Notify Jill of the reorder information by printing the output range. After printing, use Range Erase to erase the **data only** from the **output** range; keep the input, criteria, and output ranges intact so they can be used each day. Print the updated Inventory Record and save it as INVENT1.

10. Fasten together all printouts for the day. Jill will look them over tomorrow morning.

DAY TWO - Tuesday, March 16.

▶ **EXERCISE 14-6**

(Use the JDAY1 journal. Leave one blank row between each days' entries. Key the date, 03/16/—, in column A and then record the day's transactions.)

1. Sold balloon bouquet (cash)
    5 mylar
    1 foil
    1 coffee mug
        Deliver

2. Sold 3 balloon arches (medium) on account to Ensey Catering.
    3 x 1 medium arch
    3 x 30 mylar
    6 x 1 weight
        Deliver

    Arches are sold for 200% of cost.

3. Paid $20 for gas for delivery van. Check #372.

    Record the check number. Gasoline is considered a miscellaneous expense.

4. Will Brothers notify us that the Stock# 7786-31 stuffed dog is no longer available.

   No money is involved, but several worksheets must be updated. Delete the reorder point and reorder amounts from the Inventory record and delete the item number and price from the Vendor file. (Move the remaining Will Brothers item numbers and prices up to fill the two empty cells in the Vendor file. Delete the empty Will Brothers row.)

5. Subtotal all accounts for the day.

6. Print the journal and then save it on disk as JDAY2.

7. Use the Day Two transaction descriptions and the printed journal to update the CUSTOM1, INVENT1, and VENDOR files. Save the updated files as CUSTOM2, INVENT2, and VENDOR2. Query the INVENT2 file for items that need to be reordered and print them for Jill. (Use the same Query ranges; simply choose Data Query Extract.) Save the files; no printing is necessary at this time.

DAY THREE - Wednesday, March 17.

▶ **EXERCISE 14-7**

(Use the JDAY2 journal.)

1. Mailed check for store rent of $1000. Check #373.

2. Mailed the following checks:
   - $80 for electricity. chk #374
   - $21 for water. chk #375
   - $105 for phone. chk #376

3. Sold balloon bouquet (charge card)
   - 2 foil
   - 3 mylar
   - 1 teddy bear @ 200% of cost
     <u>Delivery</u>

4. Received a letter from Novelty Wholesale. The new contact person for our territory is Elaine Warren.

5. Jill placed an ad in the community newspaper.

   The newspaper will bill her for $55.

   Affects Acc Pay and Misc accounts.

6. Subtotal all accounts for the day. Save the journal as JDAY3 and then print it.

7. Update the VENDOR2 and INVENT2 files and then save them as VENDOR3 and INVENT3; it is not necessary to print them. As always, query for items to be reordered and print the information for Jill.

DAY FOUR - March 18.

> **EXERCISE 14-8**

(Use the JDAY3 journal)

1. Received payment of $27.26 on account from customer Sean Tuttle.

2. Sold large balloon arch (cash)
   60 mylar balloons
   6 weights

3. Received 10 flowers in balloon for store promotion on account from Balloonmania.

   Affects Purchases and Accounts Payable accounts.

4. Subtotal all journal accounts for the day. Save the journal as JDAY4. Do NOT print the journal until completed tomorrow.

5. Record all of today's changes to the INVENT3 Inventory Record. Then query the database for items to be reordered. Save the file as INVENT4.

6. Jill wants you to change the Inventory Record database. First, make Vend # the **second** column, right after Stock #. Next, sort the worksheet on the Stock # field (ascending). Replace the INVENT4 file. Reset the Data Query Input range to cells A5..I18.

7. Update the CUSTOM2 file and then save it as CUSTOM4. No files are printed today except the reorder information for Jill.

DAY FIVE - March 19.

> **EXERCISE 14-9**

(Use the JDAY4 journal.)

1. Wrote salary checks.
   $50 to you #377
   $300 to Jill #378

2. Sold one balloon bouquet (charge).
   1 foil
   2 confetti
   1 2-lb. chocolates
     Deliver

3. Sold balloons. Hattie of Parties To Go paid half and put half on account.
   80 mylar balloons
   10 weights

   This transaction affects three journal accounts.

4. Subtotal each journal account for the day. Save the journal as JDAY5, print it, and leave it on your screen for the next task.

5. Leave a blank line below the Subtotals line for 03/19 and key the label TOTALS FOR THE WEEK in column C. Calculate a weekly total for each journal account by adding the daily subtotals.

6. Below the totals, add a line labeled BALANCE BROUGHT FORWARD.

The amounts in this row are calculated by adding the balances brought forward from last week (row 5) to the totals for this week.

7. Print the weekly journal with page breaks so that each day is on a separate page; use the main headings and column headings as row borders; and include headers with page numbers. (Do not include the border rows in your print range, or you will get double borders.) The weekly totals and balances brought forward will appear at the end of the page with Friday's entries. Save the final journal on disk as JR0319—. Replace hyphens with current year. Use it for the following task.

8. In a blank area of the journal worksheet, key the five dates for the week. Beside each date, key the Sales subtotal for that date. Create a bar graph and a pie graph based on these daily sales Subtotal amounts. Identify each bar/pie piece and include titles with each graph. (With five days in the week, you will have five bars and five pieces of pie.) Name the graphs SALESBAR and SALESPIE. **If using 1-2-3 Release 2.x, save the graphs as SALESBAR.PIC and SALESPIE.PIC.** Print the graphs. Save the journal as JR0319— using Replace.

9. Sort the CUSTOM4 database on the Balance field in descending order and then print it and save it as CUSTOM5.

10. Record today's changes in the INVENT4 Inventory Record. No items need to be ordered today. Save the file as INVENT5.

11. Print the INVENT5 and the VENDOR3 files and then save VENDOR3 as VENDOR5.

12. Complete an Income Statement similar to the one following. Format for currency. Print the statement and save it as INCSTMT. Gather data from the Weekly Totals in the general journal. Listed below are some of the calculations:

    Cost of sales = 50% of Sales
    Gross profit = Sales - Cost of sales
    Net profit = Gross profit - Total expenses.

13. Fasten together all papers generated today.

INCOME STATEMENT
WEEK OF MARCH 15-21, 19—

INCOME
    SALES   XXX
    COST OF SALES   XXX
    GROSS PROFIT   XXX

EXPENSES
    SALARIES   XXX
    RENT   XXX
    UTILITIES   XXX
    MISCELLANEOUS   XXX
TOTAL EXPENSES   XXX

NET PROFIT   XXX

FILES CREATED IN THIS LESSON

CUSTOM
CUSTOM1
CUSTOM2
CUSTOM4
CUSTOM5
VENDOR
VENDOR2
VENDOR3
VENDOR5
INVENT
INVENT1
INVENT2
INVENT3
INVENT4
INVENT5
JOURTEMP
JR0315—
JR0319—
JDAY1
JDAY2
JDAY3
JDAY4
JDAY5
(Release 2.x: SALESBAR.PIC)
(Release 2.x: SALESPIE.PIC)
INCSTMT

Appendix

LOTUS 1-2-3 FUNCTIONS, SPECIAL KEYS, AND COMMANDS

FUNCTIONS

@AVG(range). Averages the contents of the cells in the range.

@COUNT(range). Counts the number of cells in the range.

@MAX(range). Displays the maximum value in the range of cells.

@MIN(range). Displays the minimum value in the range of cells.

@REPEAT(character string,number). Repeats the character string the specified number of times.

@SUM(range). Adds the contents of the cells in the range.

FUNCTION KEYS

F1	Help	Alt-F1	Compose
F2	Edit	Alt-F2	Step (2.x) Record (3.x)
F3	Name	Alt-F3	Run
F4	Abs(olute)	Alt-F4	Undo
F5	Goto	Alt-F5	Learn (2.x)
F6	Window	Alt-F6	Zoom (3.x)
F7	Query	Alt-F7	App1
F8	Table	Alt-F8	App2
F9	Calc	Alt-F9	App3
F10	Graph	Alt-F10	Add-in

LABEL PREFIX CHARACTERS

"   Right alignment.

'   Left alignment.

^   Center alignment.

SPECIAL KEYS

/	Activates the command menu.
\	Begins repeat characters.
?	Substitute for one unknown character in a label when querying.
*	Substitute for unknown characters at the end of a label when querying.
#	Places the page number in a header or footer.
|	Aligns items on the right, left, or center of a header or footer.
~	When it precedes a label used as selection criteria, 1-2-3 will find all occurrences except that one.
@	Places the current date in a header or footer.
Ctrl-Break	Cancels an entire command.
Cursor keys	Move the pointer up, down, left, and right.
Delete	Erases characters when in Edit mode.
End	Used with a cursor key to go to the farthest point of the worksheet/Moves the pointer to the last row or column of the worksheet/Moves the pointer to the last matching record in Query Find.
Enter	Chooses a command/Ends the Query Find operation.
Esc	Cancels current keying /Moves one step back in a command/Cancels an anchor/Ends the Query Find operation.
F6	Clears a dialog box from view in Releases 2.3 and 2.4.
Home	Returns the pointer to cell A1/Moves the pointer to the first matching record in Query Find.
Insert	Used to strikeover characters when in Edit mode.
Page Down	Moves the pointer down to the next screenful of cells.
Page Up	Moves the pointer up to the next screenful of cells.
Shift-Tab	Moves the pointer left to the next screenful of cells.
Tab	Moves the pointer right to the next screenful of cells.
↑ or ↓	Moves the pointer to other matching records in Query Find.
→ or ←	Moves the pointer among fields in the current matching record in Query Find.

COMMANDS

Copy Copies data from one place to another, leaving the data in both places.

Data Fill Enters a sequence of values in a range.

Data Query
- Delete — Deletes records that meet specific criteria.
- Extract — Finds records that meet the stated criteria and copies entire records or specified fields to the output range.
- Find — Locates records in the input range that match specified criteria.

Data Sort Arranges records in alphabetical or numerical order.
- Reset — Clears the data-range and the primary and secondary sort key settings from the previous sort.

File
- Directory — With drive and path, sets a temporary directory for storing worksheet files.
- Retrieve — Brings an existing worksheet into main memory.
- Save — Stores a worksheet on disk.
- Save Replace — Stores an edited file on disk, overwriting the original file.

Graph
- A-F — Used to set data ranges.
- Save — Saves the current graph in a file for printing or use in other programs.
- Type — Sets the type of graph, such as line, bar, or pie.
- X — Establishes the range for the X labels.

Graph Name
- Create — Gives a name to a worksheet graph so it can be used later.
- Use — Retrieves a named graph, making it the current graph.

Graph Options
    Legend   Creates legends for data ranges.
    Titles   Displays up to two identifying lines of text at the top of the graph.

Move   Places a range of cells in a new location, leaving the former location empty.

Print Image
    Current   Prints the current graph (in Release 3.x.)
    Named-Graph Prints a named graph.

Print Printer
    Align Go   Prints a basic worksheet.
    Clear All   Returns printer options to their defaults.
    Page   Ejects a sheet of paper when printing.
    Range   Defines the area of the worksheet to print.

Print Printer Options
    Advanced Layout Pitch Compressed   In Rel. 3.x, sets the print to condensed.
    Borders   Sets row or column headings to print on every page of a document.
    Footer   Prints footer information at the bottom of each page.
    Header   Prints header information at the top of each page.
    Margins   Sets left, right, top, or bottom margins; also clears all margin settings.
    Other As-Displayed   Prints the worksheet as displayed; returns the printing of a worksheet to normal after printing cell formulas.
    Other Cell-Formulas   Prints the contents of cells, as well as width and formatting codes.

Quit Yes   Exits 1-2-3 without storing the worksheet.

Range
    Erase   Erases the contents of one cell or a range of cells.
    Format   Individually formats one numeric cell or a range of numeric cells.
    Label   Aligns a range of labels.

Undo   A feature that can reverse the most recent worksheet operation.

Worksheet

Column Set-Width	Narrows or widens a column.
Delete	Deletes rows or columns from a worksheet.
Erase Yes	Erases a worksheet from the screen.
Insert	Adds rows or columns to a worksheet.

Worksheet Global

Column-Width	Widens every worksheet column the same distance. It is overridden by the Worksheet Column Set-Width command.
Default Directory	With drive and path, Update, and Quit, sets a permanent directory for storing worksheet files.
Format	Changes the default format for the entire worksheet. It is overridden by the Range Format command.

Worksheet Page

Places a page break in the worksheet.

Worksheet Titles

Clear	Unfreezes frozen titles.
Horizontal	Freezes the display of one or more rows so they remain visible at all times as the worksheet scrolls.
Vertical	Freezes the display of one or more columns so they remain visible at all times as the worksheet scrolls.

Worksheet Window

Clear	Restores the worksheet display to one window.
Horizontal	Splits the worksheet display horizontally at the pointer position.
Vertical	Splits the worksheet display vertically at the pointer position.

Glossary

Absolute cell address An address that will remain intact when copied; it is recognized by dollar signs in front of the column letter and row number.

Absolute copy When a function or formula contains an absolute cell address, the absolute cell address will remain constant when the function or formula is copied.

Anchor Establish the first cell in a range by pressing the period key.

Argument A list shown inside parentheses of the data on which a function will be performed.

Ascending order Arrangement of data with letters going from A to Z and numbers from lowest to highest.

Bar graph A graph that compares individual values or sets of values to one another.

Border Row or column headings printed on every page.

Cell The intersection of a column and a row for keying data.

Cell address The column letter and row number that identify a cell.

Cell formulas The term used to refer to line-by-line printing of the contents of cells in a worksheet.

Character string A group of characters enclosed in quote marks.

Column A vertical portion of a worksheet.

Column border A line of letters across the top of a worksheet that identifies each column.

Comma format The display of numbers with thousands, millions, and billions separated by commas; parentheses or a minus sign for negatives; and a leading zero for decimal values.

Command menu A method of command selection that displays commands and their sub commands.

Condensed print Smaller than normal printed characters, often between 16 and 18 characters per inch.

Constant Unchanging.

Contents line The top left corner of the Control Panel that displays the current cell address and the contents and format of the current cell.

Control panel The top three lines of the 1-2-3 screen, which contain the current cell address, the contents and other characteristics of the current cell, and current operating mode.

Criteria A set of labels, values, or formulas on which 1-2-3 will base a selection decision.

Criteria range Set with the Data Query Criteria command, this range specifies the search fields and the search criteria.

Criterion A single label, value, or formula on which 1-2-3 will base a selection decision.

Currency format The display of numbers with dollar signs; numbers with thousands, millions, and billions separated by commas; parentheses or a minus sign for negatives; and a leading zero for decimal values.

Current Cell The cell that the pointer is on.

Cursor keys The keys that move the pointer: →, ←, ↑, ↓.

Database Software that enables a person to enter data records, arrange them alphabetically or numerically, select only certain records, and print the data in the desired form.

Data management The function of a spreadsheet program that sorts, searches, and selects records.

Data range The series of rows or columns to be included in a graph.

Data-range The part of the Data Sort command that includes the range of records to be sorted.

Default A specification set in a software package that is often modified by the user.

Descending order Arrangement of data with letters going from Z to A and numbers from highest to lowest.

Dialog box A screen that shows the current settings associated with a task such as printing.

DOS platform Software that uses the DOS operating system but does not use Windows.

Drive The letter that designates the disk on which a worksheet will be saved. Common drives are A, B, and C.

Edit A feature that allows a file to be changed by adding, deleting, or replacing data.

Edit mode The 1-2-3 feature, obtained by pressing the F2 key, that allows correction of a cell's contents through the actions of overstrike, delete, and insert.

Enable Turn on, or activate, a feature.

Enhanced keyboard A keyboard that contains a separate numeric keypad and cursor movement keys.

Exploding pie piece A piece of pie that is separated from the other pieces for emphasis.

Field Usually a column in a spreadsheet, it contains a type of data described by a field name.

Field name Usually a column heading in a spreadsheet, it describes the field contained in that column.

File extension The additional characters preceded by a period that may be added to a file name. The 1-2-3 program automatically adds its own file extension to worksheet files so that they are easily located.

First title The first line of text at the top of a graph that identifies the graph.

Fixed format The display of numbers with a minus sign for negatives and a leading zero for decimal values.

Footer Information that appears at the bottom of each printed page.

Formula A 1-2-3 statement used to calculate numbers, other formulas, or the contents of cells.

Function A 1-2-3 built-in shortcut for complex formulas and other types of operations.

Function key A key that performs special functions in various software packages. A function key is printed with the letter *F* followed by a number, such as F3, F7, etc.

Function key template A strip of paper with the function key numbers and their commands that can be placed above or to the side of the function keys.

Function name The word after the @ sign that determines the type of function to be performed.

Global The part of a command that tells 1-2-3 to apply the command to the entire worksheet.

Goto The 1-2-3 feature that allows quick movement to a specific cell when the F5 key is pressed and followed with a cell address.

Graph A visual image of lines, bars, or segments of a circle obtained from worksheet data.

Grid lines Horizontal lines that begin at each data point on the Y-axis or vertical lines that begin at each data point on the X-axis.

Header Information that appears at the top of each printed page.

HLCO graph Tracks changes in high, low, closing, and opening prices of stocks or similar uses.

Home key This key returns the pointer to cell A1.

Home position Cell A1.

Icon panel Pictures of screen scroll arrows and a question mark for Help that is displayed on the worksheet screen for mouse users beginning with 1-2-3 Release 2.3.

Input range Set with the Data Query Input command, this range specifies the range of the database.

Label   A text entry.

Label prefix character   A character that precedes a label, determining the label's alignment in a cell.

Legend   A caption that identifies each data range.

Line graph   A graph that plots change over time.

Main command   Any of the commands that appear on the first line of commands when the command menu is first activated.

Mixed graph   A graph that combines lines and bars in the same graph.

Mode indicator   The upper right corner of the control panel that displays the current operating mode.

Monochrome monitor   A computer display with only one background color and one character color, such as white characters on a black background.

Mouse pointer   The small rectangle that is displayed in addition to the cell pointer when a mouse is available; it is used to choose commands, select cells, and make selections on the icon panel.

Num Lock key   This key must be activated for the numeric pad to indicate numbers to the computer.

Numeric keypad   A separate pad of numeric/cursor movement keys on an enhanced keyboard. The Num Lock key must be activated for the numeric keypad to indicate numbers.

Numeric symbol   The only character besides a digit that can be keyed as the first character in a numeric cell. The numeric symbols are plus, minus, decimal point, and parenthesis.

Order of operations   The sequence of calculations used to solve a mathematical problem.

Output range   Set with the Data Query Output command, this range determines where copies of selected records will be placed.

Override   Dominate or set aside, as a range command overrides a global command.

Overstrike   The replacement of a character with another character.

Page break   The position where one printed page ends and a new one begins.

Path   The directory or sequence of directories that indicates where 1-2-3 is to save a worksheet.

Percent format   The display of numbers as percentages.

Pie graph   A graph that identifies the relationship of each value in a data range to the entire data range.

"Playing what if"   Keying a value to see what effect it has on other values in a spreadsheet; it is used for decision making.

Point to cells   The process of moving the pointer to each cell as a formula is being constructed.

Pointer   Name for the 1-2-3 cursor.

Primary-key   The first field on which records will be sorted.

PrintGraph   A program utility that ships with Lotus 1-2-3 Rel. 2.x to enable the printing of graphs.

Program   A series of instructions telling the computer what actions to take.

Query   A question or inquiry. In 1-2-3, you inquire whether particular records exist in a database.

Range   A rectangular group of adjacent cells.

Record   Usually a row in a spreadsheet, it contains all related fields about an individual or event.

Relative copy   When a function or formula containing cell addresses is copied, the addresses copy relative to the new row or column in which the formula or function is placed.

Repeat characters   The feature used to fill a cell with one or more characters.

Row   A horizontal portion of the worksheet.

Row border The line of numbers going down the left edge of the worksheet that identifies each row.

Scale indicator The part of a graph that shows the units, such as thousands or millions, of the Y-axis.

Scientific notation A short numeric expression used by 1-2-3 to display a value when the normal display of the value is too wide for the cell.

Scroll The movement of the screen as you move the pointer in a larger worksheet.

Scroll arrows The arrows on the mouse icon panel that can be used to move the pointer.

Second title The second line of text at the top of a graph that identifies the graph.

Secondary-key The second field on which records will be sorted.

Shading value The color or the hatch patterns obtained from the B range of a pie graph.

Software package An application program offered as a complete system, which usually includes a program on disk and manuals for using the program.

Sort Arrange in order, alphabetically or numerically.

Sort order The arrangement of records in ascending or descending order.

Spill over The ability of a long label to use blank cells on the right for additional display space.

Spreadsheet Application software that calculates, automatically updates related figures, and usually provides graphical images of numeric data.

Stack bar graph Compares individual and total values by stacking various bars on top of each other in a single bar.

Standard keyboard A keyboard that does not have a separate numeric pad and cursor movement keys.

Status Line The display line below the worksheet that displays the date and time or the name of the current worksheet.

Strikeover The replacement of one character with another character.

Sub command A command that is available because of the previous command that was chosen.

Titles This command freezes the display of one or more rows and/or columns, ensuring they are visible at all times.

Toggle A key that is pressed to turn a feature on or off.

Value Display on the mode indicator when a number, formula, or function is being entered.

Wildcards The * and ? characters that may be substituted for unknown characters in a label used as search criteria.

Window This command splits the worksheet display, allowing a view of two parts of the worksheet simultaneously.

Worksheet The name for a 1-2-3 spreadsheet.

X-axis The line at the bottom of a graph with horizontal data points.

X-axis title Text that describes the X-axis.

X label Characters that describe a data point on the X-axis.

XY graph A graph that shows a relationship between two types of numeric data.

Y-axis The line along the left side of a graph with vertical data points.

Y-axis title Text that describes the Y-axis.

Y label A number on the Y-axis that describes a data point.

Index

A

Absolute cell address 131, 222
Absolute copy 131, 222
Add characters 57
Advanced Applications—
 Balloon Biz 203
Advanced printing 95
Anchor 68, 222
Appearance of numbers 31
Appendix 217
Argument 222
Ascending order 143, 222
@ Avg function 69
@ Count 71
@ Max function 70
@ Min function 69
@ Repeat 72
@ Sum function 66

B

Back out of or cancel a command 20
Backup 42
Bar graph 185, 222
Basic printing 44
Border 13, 101, 222
 column 13, 222
 row 13, 224

C

Calculating with
 cell values 55
 numbers 54
Cancel 42
 or back out of a command 20
Caps lock 18
Cell 13, 222
Cell address, 13, 222
 absolute 131, 222
Cell formulas 99, 222

Change the default drive 33
Changing the worksheet
 with copy and repeat characters 125
 move, insert, and delete 109
Character string 222
Choosing a command 20
Clear print settings 103
Column(s) 222
 and rows 13
 border 13, 222
 insert rows and 112
Comma format 83, 222
Command menu 19, 222
Commands 219
Condensed print 97, 222
Constant 131, 222
Constructing a function 66
Contents line 18, 222
Control panel 18, 222
Correcting errors 27
Criteria 158, 222
Criteria range 156, 222
Criterion 160, 222
Critical thinking project
 3 40
 5 64
 7 94
 9 124
 11 154
 13 202
Currency format 83, 222
Current cell 13, 222
Cursor keys 14, 222
Customer database 204

D

Daily procedure 209
Database 3, 222
Data fill 168
Data management 222
Data query 155
 and data fill 155

 criteria 156
 delete 164
 extract 156, 165
 find 158
 input 156
 output 156
 steps 157
 unique 156
Data range 176, 222
Data-range 143, 223
Data sort reset 149
Default 223
Delete
 characters 58
 rows and columns 114
Descending order 143, 223
Dialog box 117, 223
DOS platform 3, 223
Drive 223

E

Edit 223
 cells 56
 mode 223
Elements of a graph 177, 178
Enable 114, 223
End 15
Enhanced keyboard 5, 223
Entering data 27
Erase 80
 a worksheet 35
Error correction chart 28
Explanation of accounts 207
Exploding pie piece 191, 223

F

Field 141, 223
Field name 142, 223
File
 directory 34
 extension 223
 retrieve 41

save 34
First title 178, 223
Fixed format 83, 223
Footer 103, 223
Footers and headers 103
Format
   comma 83, 222
   currency 83, 222
   fixed 83, 223
   of labels 88
   of numbers 82
   percent 83, 224
Formula 51, 53, 223
Function 65, 217, 223
Function key(s) 6, 217, 223
   and 1-2-3 6
   template 223
Function name 223

G

General journal 207
Global 223
   column width 89
   format 84
Glossary 222
Goto 15, 223
Graph(s), 3, 175, 176, 223
   bar 185, 222
   elements of 177, 178
   HLCO 223
   line 179, 224
   mixed 224
   multiple bar 185, 187
   name a 183
   pie 191, 224
   reset 191
   save 183
   single bar 185
   stack bar 185, 189, 225
   types of 176, 177
Graph name
   create 183
   use 183
Grid lines 178, 223

H

Header 103, 223
Headers and footers 103
Help 21
HLCO graph 223

Home 14
   key 223
   position 14, 223

I

Icon panel 16, 223
Input range 156, 223
Insert rows and columns 112
Instructions for using this book 6
Introduction to spreadsheets 1
Inventory record 206

K

Keyboards
   and 1-2-3 5
   enhanced 5, 223
   standard 5, 225

L

Label 28, 224
   prefix character 29, 217, 224
   that begins with a number 29
Legend 178, 224
Line graph 179, 224
Load 1-2-3 12
Lotus 1-2-3 functions, special keys, and commands 217

M

Main command 19, 224
Mixed graph 224
Mode indicator 18, 224
Monochromatic monitor 224
Mouse 6
   actions 16
   pointer 16, 224
Mouse, using the 16
Move 109
Move what? range 110
Moving the pointer 14
Multiple bar graph 185, 187

N

Name a graph 183

Num lock key 5, 18, 224
Numbers, 31
   appearance of 31
   and numeric symbols, using 51
Numeric cell that is too narrow 52
Numeric keypad 5, 224
Numeric symbol, 31, 224
   and numbers, using 51

O

1-2-3,
   as a database 141
   function keys and 6
   how calculates 3
   keyboards and 5
   load 12
   Lotus functions, special keys, and commands 217
      Lotus spreadsheet 3
   quit 35
Options
   backup 42
   cancel 42
   print 44
   replace 42
Order
   ascending 143, 222
   descending 143, 223
   of operations 4, 224
Output range 156, 224
Override 224
Overstrike 57, 224

P

Page
   break 100, 224
   down 14
   up 14
Path 224
Percent format 83, 224
Perform the sort 144
Permanent directory 34
Pie graph 191, 225
"Playing what if" 3, 224
Point to cells 224
Pointer, 13, 224
   moving the 14
Pointing 55

Preparing the database for
   query 156
Primary-key 143, 224
Print 44
Print cell formulas 98
Print clear command choices
   104
PrintGraph 193, 224
Print image
   current 193
   –named graph 193
Print options
   borders 101
   footer 103
   header 103
   margins 96
   other cell formulas 99
Program 2, 224

Q

Query 156, 224
   delete 164
   extract 165
   find 158
Quit 22
Quit 1-2-3 35

R

Range 44, 79, 224
   and global format 79
   erase 80
   format 83, 85
   label 88
Range,
   criteria 156, 222
   data 176, 222
   input 156, 223
   move what? 110
   output 156, 224
   to where? 110
Record 141, 224
Relative 129
   copy 129, 224
Repeat characters 133, 224
Replace 42
Replace a worksheet 42
   with a new name 42
   with the same name 42
Reset, 149
   data sort 149

Retrieve
   a work sheet 41
   and print 41
Row(s), 224
   borders 13, 225
   insert columns and 112

S

Save a
   graph 183
   worksheet 34, 183
Scale indicator 178, 225
Scientific notation 225
Scroll 225
   arrows 16, 225
   lock 18
Search for labels 162
Second title 178, 225
Secondary-key 143, 147, 225
Secondary sort 147
Shading value 225
Shift-tab 14
Single bar graph 185
Software package 225
Sort 142, 225
   key 143
   order 143, 225
Sorting 141, 143
Special
   characters 52
   keys 218
Spill over 29, 225
Spreadsheet(s), 2, 225
   introduction to 1
   why used 2
Stack bar graph 185, 189, 225
Standard keyboard 5, 225
Status line 13, 225
Strikeover 227
Sub command 19, 225

T

Tab 14
Temporary directory 34
Titles 118, 225
Toggle 13, 225
To where? range 110
Types of graphs 176, 177

U

Undo 114
Using
   numbers and numeric
      symbols 51
   the mouse 16

V

Value 227
Vendor database 205
Viewing with windows and
   titles 116

W

Why spreadsheets are used 2
Wide worksheets 95
Wildcards 162, 225
Window 116, 225
Worksheet, 12, 225
   column set-width 32
   delete 114
   global column-width 89
   global default directory 34
   global format 83, 84
   insert 112
   page 100
   screen and command menu
      11
   titles clear 118
   window 116
   window clear 117

X

X-axis 178, 225
X-axis title 178, 225
X-label 178, 225
XY graph 225

Y

Y-axis 178, 225
Y-axis title 178, 225
Y-label 178, 225
Your new position 203